You Have the Right to Know Your Rights

What Teens Should Know

ISSUES IN FOCUS TODAY

Maurene J. Hinds

Enslow Publishers, Inc.

40 Industrial Road	PO Box 38
Box 398	Aldershot
Berkeley Heights, NJ 07922	Hants GU12 6BP
USA	UK

http://www.enslow.com

Copyright © 2005 by Maurene J. Hinds

Library of Congress Cataloging-in-Publication Data

Hinds, Maurene J.
    You have the right to know your rights : what teens should know /
Maurene J. Hinds.
        p. cm. — (Issues in focus today)
    Includes bibliographical references and index.
    ISBN 0-7660-2358-3
    1. Teenagers—Legal status, laws, etc.—United States—Juvenile literature.
2. Children's rights—United States—Juvenile literature. 3. Minors—United States—
Juvenile literature. I. Title. II. Series.
    KF479.Z9H56 2005
    342.7308'772—dc22

                                                                2005011822

Printed in the United States of America

10 9 8 7 6 5 4 3 2 1

To Our Readers:
We have done our best to make sure all Internet Addresses in this book were active and
appropriate when we went to press. However, the author and the publisher have no
control over and assume no liability for the material available on those Internet sites
or on other Web sites they may link to. Any comments or suggestions can be sent by
e-mail to comments@enslow.com or to the address on the back cover.

Illustration Credits: AP/Wide World, p. 54; BananaStock, pp. 52, 79; Corbis Images
Royalty-Free, pp. 1, 3, 34, 66, 74, 95; Digital Stock, p. 87; Digital Vision, pp. 5, 63, 89;
EyeWire Images, p. 37; Hemera Image Express, pp. 3, 8, 13, 26, 29, 70, 84, 93; Library
of Congress, p. 31; photo by Drake Mabry, copyright 1965, the Des Moines Register
and Tribune Company, reprinted with permission, p. 17; National Archives, pp. 3, 11;
Photos.com, pp. 3, 23, 39, 43, 45, 59, Rubberball Productions, p. 50; Stockbyte Images,
p. 77, 82.

Cover Illustration: Photos.com (background); BananaStock (small photo); Corbis Images
Royalty-Free (large photograph). Though many students think of their lockers as private
property, the courts have held that they can be searched in most circumstances.

Contents

In 2002, thirteen-year-old Mitch Muller borrowed a friend's laser pointer key chain for a few minutes while in class. He shined the red light around the classroom. Then he returned the toy to his friend.

Those couple of minutes cost Mitch a year of school. The school expelled Mitch (and two of his friends) for a year. He went to a school for troubled teens until he could return to his regular school. The school officials said the toy looked like a small gun.

The expulsions were a result of the Colorado school's zero-tolerance policy. The school had "zero tolerance" for dangerous weapons. This included anything that looked like a weapon. Part of a key chain was an orange laser pointer about two and a half inches long. The teacher thought it looked like a gun. The school "stuck to its guns" when pressured by Mitch's parents. It did not change the decision.

Mitch's parents fought the decision. They paid thousands of dollars in legal fees. In June 2004, a district court judge ruled that the school should remove the incident from Mitch's record.

Were Mitch's rights violated? The school officials did not think so. The school's rules were clear. The school would not tolerate anything that looked like a weapon. To the teacher, the laser pointer looked like a small gun. Mitch's parents did not agree. They fought against the ruling and eventually won.[1]

Minors are people under the age of eighteen. In most states in the United States, eighteen is the age at which minors become adults, with most legal rights. These include the right to vote and to serve in the armed forces. Other rights also become legal at this age, such as the right to enter into a contract.

Certain basic rights are sometimes called "human rights." These have less to do with the law. These are what some people think are rights basic to all humanity. An example is the right to live in a dignified manner. For example, many people do not consider slavery to fit the definition of "dignified." As a result, many people think slavery is a serious violation of human rights.

This book discusses issues about both legal rights and human rights. It also covers a number of questions related to rights. Do minors have rights? Should they have rights? If so, which ones? Who controls those rights? Is it lawful and ethical (good or right in conduct) to restrict rights to persons under eighteen?

Until fairly recently, children had almost no rights, even in the United States. The law considered children property of their parents. This meant that parents could treat their children however they saw fit. This could include physical harm. Parents could hit their children or even sell them into slavery. Over time, however, parents and others began to see children as people. They saw that children had rights and were not property. Still, many children around the world do not have the same rights as children in the United States.

Throughout history, issues of human rights have evolved. This can be seen in examples of uprisings against oppressors, revolutions, and wars. The United States' history grew out of the oppression the founders tried to escape. The Revolutionary War released the colonists from British rule. Later, the slavery of African Americans became an issue of human rights and led to the Civil War. Over time, the Industrial Revolution gave rise to many

> **Until fairly recently, children had almost no rights, even in the United States. The law considered children property of their parents.**

changes in the way Americans did business. Dangerous work and extremely long working hours led workers to revolt and demand changes. The world discovered Hitler's horrors during the Second World War. After this, human rights became even more of an issue around the world.

In 1948, the United Nations developed the Universal Declaration of Human Rights (UDHR). This listed what the organization considered to be basic human rights. This included the right to life, security, freedom of expression, and education. The articles of the declaration are not law. They do serve as a guide for all nations on human rights issues. But not all nations agree that these are basic human rights. Even people in the United States do not all agree on what human rights are or should be. Those nations that agree with the declarations set forth by the United Nations pledge their support by, first, signing the articles. After signing, they ratify them, meaning they formally and legally agree to the articles.

Under some zero-tolerance policies, students can be punished for anything resembling gunplay.

Some critics argue that the UDHR was developed from ideas out of Western culture. They argue that the articles do not consider Eastern countries' ideals. The articles are supposed to be universal. But many of the rights listed actually go against some people's views on government. Some Asian countries, for example, place a high emphasis on societal values rather than individual values. But some of the rights in the UDHR promote individual rights first. This is offensive to those who place higher values on societal rights. The United States has criticized China for its human rights violations. One famous example occurred in 1989 in Tiananmen Square, Beijing. A group of university students protested against the Communist government. They wanted democratic reform. After about a month and a half of protest, the Chinese government used the army to clear out the demonstrators. As the students left the square, violence erupted in the streets. The police killed many protesters. Some critics of the UDHR argue that many Western countries still have human rights violations of their own to correct. These critics would like to see a human rights agenda that is more universal.

John Shattuck, a former U.S. assistant secretary of state, wrote an article called "Civil and Political Rights in the United States." In it, he says, "Human rights have come to be recognized as the universal birthright of every man, woman, and child on this planet."[2] On November 20, 1989, the United Nations adopted the Convention on the Rights of the Child (CRC). This outlined specific rights for children around the world. The CRC defines children as anyone under the age of eighteen. The Convention lists fifty-four articles about children's rights and how to put the rights into action. (Two other optional rules added later deal with children in the armed forces and child pornography.) The articles include discrimination issues and the right of children to speak out on their own behalf. It says children should be able to voice opinions on what is best for them. The United States signed the convention, but the Senate did not vote to ratify the articles. (Somalia is the only other country that has not ratified the CRC.) There are a few reasons for this. One reason is that the United States has traditionally placed a high level of importance on the rights of parents to determine what is best for their children. The United States argues that a set of rules may interfere with a parent's right to make decisions.

Another reason the United States did not ratify the CRC is that the articles say that the death penalty for anyone under eighteen years of age is a violation of human rights. Before 2005, some states allowed the execution of minors; other states did not. Then, in March, the Supreme Court held, in *Roper* v.

Simmons, that executing minors was unconstitutional. It is not yet known whether this change will affect the U.S. position on the CRC.

Other reasons the United States refused to ratify the CRC include the convention's policies on economic, social, and cultural rights. The United States has long recognized political rights (such as free expression and the right to assemble). But it has been slower in recognizing issues such as the right to education, health care, and decent standards of living.[3] People in the United States continue to debate these issues. While there is no formal "right" to an education, for example, minors must attend school up to a particular age. This age varies by state—which leads to the final issue of why the United States has not ratified the CRC.

Each state is responsible for making its own laws, as long as those laws do not violate the Constitution. Because of this, many laws vary from state to state. If the government ratified the CRC, the states would have less power to determine their own laws. This goes against how the United States government is set up.

Why focus on children's rights? Many human rights groups treat children's rights as its own issue for one reason: to give children a voice. Some children are stuck in abusive situations or poverty, or are forced to work against their will. Someone needs to speak out for them because children cannot do it for themselves. Many violations of children's rights still occur around the world today. Some continue in the United States. The issue of children's rights is very big and covers the globe. This book focuses on the rights of minors in the United States. Even here, the issues are many and cannot be covered in one book. This book is a sampling of some of the issues that have faced children and adolescents in the United States. It also discusses laws that have come from or changed children's rights issues, and the current state of these issues.

In the United States, children worked in factories up through the early twentieth century. This little girl was photographed in a North Carolina mill in 1908.

Constitutional Rights

The Bill of Rights protects citizens' rights in the United States. These are the first ten amendments to the U.S. Constitution. Additional amendments have been added over the years. Each state also has its own constitution, which must not be in violation of the U.S. Constitution. Many cases involving constitutional rights result in litigation (a lawsuit). The state and federal courts decide most cases. However, the only purpose of the United States Supreme Court is to deal with cases involving the Constitution. If a person is not happy with a decision of a state's highest court, he or she may ask the Supreme Court to hear the case.

This can only be done if the issue is one that is directly related to the U.S. Constitution. Some laws are different from state to state. These include laws that affect human rights issues. In these situations, the Supreme Court may refuse to hear the cases because it feels they should be decided at the state level.

How does this process work? The Supreme Court reviews the lower court's decision. It then decides if it will hear arguments on the case. Nine justices sit on the Supreme Court. Each justice votes on the issue at hand. A majority vote will determine the case. If the justices do not all agree, each side will write a statement, an opinion, stating their reasons. Often one justice will write this, speaking on behalf of the others on the same side. Sometimes more than one justice will write an opinion. This depends on his or her views on the subject. The Supreme Court does not act like other courts. There is no jury and no witnesses testify. Arguments for or against a person's innocence are not presented. Lawyers only argue whether or not a person's constitutional rights have been violated.

State courts have decided many cases involving children's rights. Sometimes these cases have prompted a change in state law. Other cases have made it all the way to the Supreme Court and brought about a change in the laws across the country.

Freedom of Expression

Many Americans say the right to express themselves is one thing they enjoy about living in this country. U.S. citizens, for example, may openly criticize the government. Citizens of some other nations are not so lucky. This type of expression may land a person in prison or even result in their being put to death in some countries.

Expressing oneself may mean many different things to different people. Some view it as the ability to say whatever they believe. To others, expression means dyeing one's hair hot pink. But whatever the view, expression has its limits. This is true even in a country that protects freedom of speech and freedom of expression.

Can a person say whatever he or she wants? Yes and no. Saying certain things may result in a problem with the law. Using swear words in public may violate a local law on disturbing the peace. Threatening to kill the president, whether in speech or in writing, is a federal offense. Other threatening speech, however, is allowed. Physical harm against another person is illegal. But U.S. citizens are able to say what some consider "hate speech." Hate speech is when a person or persons express hatred toward another group of people. Many regard hate speech as offensive. But it is still legal in many cases. People have the right to their opinions and to express those opinions. It does not matter how others may feel about those opinions.

"Defamation of character" is the legal term that describes when one person tells lies about another person that are intended to damage that person's reputation or otherwise cause harm. The defamed person has the right to sue the person who is saying the slanderous or false things.

The First Amendment does not protect threatening speech. This is speech that contains threats against a person or a person's property. In these cases, lawyers try to show in court that most people would consider the speech a serious intent to do bodily harm or assault. Then the person making the threats may be found guilty of breaking the law.

Expressing oneself through personal appearance also has some limits. How a person chooses to physically express him or herself seems almost limitless. The law, however, does draw the line with some behaviors. These include showing parts of the body in public (women's breasts or either gender's genitals) and some sexual conduct.

Religious expression also has some limits. The founders of the United States wanted to make sure the government did not officially support any religion. As a result, U.S. citizens enjoy the freedom to practice any form of religion. As with all rights, religious expression is okay so long as it does not violate another person's rights, well-being, or health. Some religious practices are illegal. This includes intentional cruelty to other people or denying medical care to a person in need.

Teens have many of the same rights of expression that adults have. But these rights are limited at school.

What Are My Rights?

Some people have argued that young people's rights should not remain outside the door when they attend school. However, public schools have the duty to ensure the safety and well-being of all students. As a result, some rights that are legal outside of school have some limits inside the classroom. This includes some rights of expression.

Students have the right to express themselves in school as long as that expression does not harm another person. It also cannot interfere with the school's goal of education. The classroom and extracurricular activities can provide a good way for students to discuss issues, express opinions, and develop a sense of identity and self. For example, in 1965, Mary Beth Tinker, thirteen, along with her brother, John, fifteen, and friend, Christopher Eckhardt, sixteen, wore a black armband to protest the war in Vietnam. The school, which had recently banned armbands, said they were a "disruptive influence" and could lead to a student protest. The school suspended all three students. Mary Beth and her family sued the school. They argued it was a violation of the students' First Amendment rights. The case, *Tinker* v. *Des Moines,* ended up in the Supreme Court. There, the justices agreed with the students that the statements of protest were not disruptive and did not violate the rights of other students. The students had First Amendment rights to express their opinions. In the words of the Court,

First Amendment rights, applied in light of the special characteristics of the school environment, are available to teachers and students. It can hardly be argued that either students or teachers shed their constitutional rights to freedom of speech or expression at the schoolhouse gate.[1]

The *Tinker* case was a controversial but important step in First Amendment rights for students. More recently, issues have come up following the Columbine school shootings, the terrorist attacks of September 11, 2001, and the recent invasion of Iraq. School officials do have the right (and responsibility) to keep order within the school. But have the ideas expressed in the *Tinker* case been forgotten? In February 2003, a school ordered a student in Dearborn, Michigan, to either take off a T-shirt or go home. The T-shirt said, "International Terrorist," and had a picture of President George W. Bush. The school argued that the shirt would "inflame the passions at the school where a majority of students are Arab-American."[2] The student chose to go home and miss school rather than change his clothes. In March 2003, a student at Leland High School in San Jose, California, wore a shirt to school that said "Bomb Saddam" on one side and "Attack Iraq" on another. The principal told him he faced suspension if he wore the shirt again.[3] Some people argue that during times of political stress or war, we must give up some personal freedoms. It may be a fine line between what starts problems at school and what may be a violation of First Amendment rights.

> Students have the right to express themselves in school as long as that expression does not harm anyone or interfere with the school's goal of education.

Some types of speech or expression are legal outside of school. But schools do not allow all types of speech. Schools do not put up with hate speech in school. The school has the power to limit it, despite a person's constitutional right to

Mary Beth Tinker's black armband resulted in her suspension from school, but her name became associated with a landmark Supreme Court case about the rights of students to express themselves.

free speech. The purpose of hate speech is to create emotions and strong reactions. Such speech in school would disturb the classroom setting and the goal of learning. And just as in the "real world," schools do not allow students to tell lies intended to harm the reputations of other students. This is true for both verbal and written remarks.

What Are the Current Laws?

Public schools have the power to decide what is okay and what is not regarding students' appearance. (Private schools have even more control in this and other areas.) Schools may ban anything they think will get in the way of the goal of learning. Various court cases have ended up with different rulings. In 1966, the case that set the tone for hairstyles in public school took place in Dallas, Texas. Phil Ferrell, Paul Jarvis, and Steve Webb were members of a rock band. They decided that growing their hair long would help to promote the band. The principal of their school, however, disagreed with this idea. He told the students they could not attend their senior year of school unless they cut their hair. The state court agreed with the principal. It ruled that the school had the authority to make the rules, not the students. If the school can show that a form of expression is getting in the way of other students' ability to learn, then the school may curb that behavior. This can include such things as wearing gang-related colors or clothing, religious symbols, or T-shirts with advertising or other messages. Schools may also limit extreme makeup or hairstyles. Some schools decide to use school uniforms to help avoid problems with clothing. If everyone is wearing the same thing, students will not be distracted by messages on T-shirts or worrying about not having the "right" clothes.

A school may not show special treatment of one particular religion over another. This is why prayer in schools has gotten so much attention. Schools may allow a moment of silence. This does not lend itself to one particular religion over another.

But reading a prayer out loud in class or over the loudspeaker is not allowed. This would be showing support of certain religious beliefs. Schools do not allow prayers at graduation ceremonies for the same reasons. Students have the right to attend school and school functions without being exposed to religious beliefs or statements.

In a 1988 case, *Hazelwood School District* v. *Kuhlmeier*, the Supreme Court ruled that a school could control the content in school newspapers. This is because they are not a forum for public expression. This particular case dealt with stories in which students expressed personal opinions about a family divorce, teen pregnancy, sexual activity, and birth control. Some of the quotes used names of the persons interviewed. While other quotes did not, students would have been able to guess the person quoted. The principal removed two pages from the paper. He decided that if the paper went to print, it would be a violation of both students' and their parents' right to privacy. The Supreme Court agreed.[4] Students may not say or write whatever they wish in school. While school papers may be an excellent source to express opinions and debate issues, some topics may be off-limits. Schools have the power to prohibit material considered improper. This power may not be in violation of students' rights.

Speaking Out

Has anyone opposed these laws? Most of the challenges to the law or school policies are the result of specific incidents. They are not the result of groups trying to change the laws in general. Most of these cases involve a person arguing a violation of his or her constitutional rights. Despite general laws, specific cases may or may not be a violation of a student's constitutional rights.

Should there be laws that forbid hate speech? Some argue yes, some argue no. Speech shown in court to be a real threat of physical harm may result in criminal charges. But under the First Amendment, people of the United States have the freedom to express their opinions. Some reasons for arguing against hate speech laws are that hate speech is too unclear and difficult to define. What one person considers hate speech may not be to another person or group. Another risk of having hate speech laws is that they may work against the minorities or victims at whom hate speech is often directed. These groups need the freedom to respond to hate directed at them. They need the freedom to make their voices heard, and to bring attention to the hate problems in the first place. Laws or restrictions against hate speech could actually have the opposite effect, opponents say.

Naturally, hate speech offends many people. Some worry that such speech will lead to actions against the targets of such speech. Hate speech gives rise to many emotions. These emotions can lead to heated arguments, physical harm, and riots. Hate speech carries a high level of emotion. It also serves to threaten the targets or bring an audience to action. Because of this, schools may limit such freedom of expression.

In 1962, the Supreme Court heard a case on prayer in the school system, *Engel* v. *Vitale*. The New York State Board of Regents had approved a prayer that students recited daily in New York schools: "Almighty God, we acknowledge our dependence upon Thee, and we beg Thy blessing upon us, our parents, our teachers and our Country."[5] The Regents

Amendment 1: Freedom of Religion, Speech, and the Press; Rights of Assembly and Petition

Congress shall make no law respecting an establishment of religion, or prohibiting the free exercise thereof; or abridging the freedom of speech, or of the press; or the right of the people peaceably to assemble, and to petition the government for a redress of grievances.

claimed that the prayer was not associated with any particular religion. Some parents in one school district decided that the prayer was unconstitutional and violated the rights of students. New York state courts first heard the case. It decided that the school system operated within its legal limits. The Supreme Court disagreed, using the Establishment Clause as part of its argument.

Schools can limit some forms of expression—such as wearing gang-related colors or clothing, religious symbols, or T-shirts with messages—if they get in the way of students' ability to learn.

The Establishment Clause is one of two clauses under the First Amendment that deal with the issue of religion and government. The amendment prohibits the government from declaring or funding any particular religion. This had happened in other countries.[6] For example, England had a long history of conflict between Protestants and Catholics. For a long time, whichever religion the ruling king or queen supported became the national religion.

In its decision on *Engel* v. *Vitale*, the Supreme Court wrote,

> The constitutional prohibition against laws respecting an establish-
> ment of religion must at least mean that in this country it is no
> part of the business of government to compose official prayers for
> any group of the American people to recite as a part of a religious
> program carried on by government.[7]

The decision was controversial then, and it continues to be so today.

Both those who support prayer in public schools and those who oppose it use the First Amendment for their argument. Those who support school prayer argue that the amendment does not allow the government to prohibit religious expression. The amendment states, in reference to religious expression, "*. . . or prohibiting the free exercise thereof.*" Those who argue against school prayer say that the government cannot encourage one religion over another. Because prayer is often associated with a particular religion, and because public schools are government-supported institutions, they say prayer should not be allowed.

In 1992, the Supreme Court decided in *Lee* v. *Weisman* that school prayers were not proper at a junior high graduation ceremony. In this case, the school had a policy that allowed for a prayer at graduation. The rules stated that the prayer needed to be nondenominational. Deborah Weisman, who graduated in 1989, did not feel that students should be forced to listen to a prayer at a school function. She and her family sued the school. The case eventually ended up in the Supreme Court. Deborah and her family won the case. The Justices ruled,

> A government may not coerce anyone to support or participate in religion or its exercise, or otherwise act in a way which "establishes a [state] religion or religious faith, or tends to do so."[8]

The Court also said,

> That the directions may have been given in a good-faith attempt to make the prayers acceptable to most persons does not resolve the dilemma caused by the school's involvement, since the government may not establish an official or civic religion as a means of avoiding the establishment of a religion with more specific creeds.[9]

The school prayer issue has come up again and again since these decisions. The debates continue. However, these rulings, at least for now, have set the standard for prayer in school.

Does this mean that no religious activities can occur on the school grounds? No. Many schools have clubs or groups that are based on students' religious beliefs. The difference is that involvement in these groups is by choice. No students are required to attend. The school's primary responsibility is to provide educational opportunities for all students. This also includes keeping order in the classroom and among the student population in general. This does not mean that hot topics cannot or will not be discussed in the classroom. Schools are a

Young people's right to express themselves through their appearance sometimes conflicts with school rules. Courts have given schools some power to restrict students' clothing and grooming choices.

great place to discuss all sides of an issue. But the school does have the right to place limits on its students.

What Can I Do If My Rights Are Being Violated?

Unfortunately, there is no one way to handle a case about freedom of expression. Each situation is different. The laws vary from state to state. For many teenagers, these events are likely to occur within the school setting, but this is not always the case. Other issues to think about are where and how suspected violations occur. For example, can a teen be banned from shopping in a grocery store owned by Hispanics if the teen made racist remarks while in the store? In this case, yes, because the store is a privately owned business. But what if the teen makes similar remarks in a public library? This may depend on the situation. If the remarks are disruptive to other patrons, then the librarians may ask a teen to leave. The patron could face suspension from using the public resource for a set amount of time. What if the conversation takes place privately and a Hispanic librarian overhears the conversation and is offended? Can the library throw out the teen? Probably not, because the conversation only took place between the two people involved.

Events like these may be treated differently than those that occur at school. If necessary, students may report an incident to the police. Often, though, people who feel their rights were violated will start by talking to a lawyer. The lawyer will then advise those involved on what actions to take. Lawyers may file a lawsuit on the person's behalf against the other party. Cases are often settled out of court through a shared agreement. Other times, however, cases go to court. These may end up in the Supreme Court.

In school, most issues will be reported to school officials or the school board. Many issues can be solved without having to pursue the matter further. Sometimes this does not work. It may be necessary to seek legal help and possibly take the case to court.

Students have as much right as anyone else to guarantee the protection of their rights, in or out of school. Students who have stood up to the rules and asked for change caused courts to support some of the rights of students. These cases brought public attention to the rights of children and teens. Not everyone agrees with the results. But it is the basis of constitutional protection that everyone has the opportunity to fight for his or her rights, regardless of age.

DONAIR
HAMBURGER
CHEESEBURGER
LARGE FRIES   3.0
MEDIUM FRIES   2.5
SMALL FRIES   2.0
LARGE POUTINE   3.7
SMALL POUTINE   2.7
HOT DOG
POGO
DRINK
CHICKEN BURGER

HAVE A NIC

3   **On the Job**

Until recently, children and teens had no rights in the
workforce. Children often worked twelve- to fifteen-hour days,
six days a week during the Industrial Revolution. The law did
not require breaks. Many children worked all day without a
rest or very short breaks. Business owners would also punish
workers who they thought were not working hard enough.
These punishments could include physical force or a cut in pay.
Children spent hours bent over machines in textile factories.
Unsafe working conditions were common. Children worked
with dangerous machinery on a regular basis. People of all ages
were seriously hurt and even died while on the job.

In the United States and several European countries, however, conditions began to change beginning in the nineteenth century. Laws now protect minors from abuses in the workplace. In many parts of the world, conditions are changing as well. Child labor issues are a major concern among human rights groups. Despite progress, child labor is still a major concern in some parts of the world.

Other laws affect all workers, not just children and teens. It is important to have an understanding of these laws before entering the workforce.

What Are My Rights?

Even before hiring someone, employers may not ask some questions either on applications or in an interview. Questions about a person's race or religion are not legal in most cases. Questions about age can also be illegal. An employer may ask if the job seeker is legally old enough to work. But employers cannot ask for a date of birth or why a person is seeking work at this age. Employers may not ask about relationship status. An employer may not ask if the applicant is seeing anyone, nor if the person is married. Employers may ask a person about prior felony convictions. But employers may not ask about a person's history of arrest or if he or she has been in trouble with the law. Many older teens may seek delivery jobs. In this case, an employer may ask if the person has a valid driver's license. An employer may also ask if an applicant is a member of any clubs or organizations that may be relevant to the job. They may not ask an applicant to list all clubs or organizations of which he or she is a member.[1]

It is also smart to read the application carefully, especially the "fine print." Applicants may be giving up some rights when signing the application. It is important to understand the agreement. And, most importantly, an applicant must never exaggerate his or her history or lie on an application.

These actions can lead to immediate firing after getting the job. This is true even if the employer does not discover the lie until after the person has worked for a long time in the position.

An employer has to fulfill certain legal duties for all employees, not just minors. These vary somewhat from state to state. But there are some similarities across the country. For example, employers must provide a safe place to work. Some jobs are hazardous. Employers must provide safety and health training and provide information on any chemicals that are used. Employers must follow the rules of OSHA. This stands for the Occupational Safety and Health Administration. This is a government agency that regulates workplace safety. Many workplaces must also provide workers' compensation insurance. This insurance covers injuries or illnesses that occur if a person is sick or injured on the job. Most jobs must also pay the minimum wage. This may not be the case with jobs such as waiting tables. Tips from customers provide a large part of the income from restaurant work.

> In many countries, laws protect minors from abuses in the workplace. But child labor is still a major concern in some parts of the world.

What Are the Current Laws?

Certain age limits determine what type of work a minor may do. Age may also determine how many hours a minor may work each week. The 1938 Fair Labor Standards Act covered some areas about child labor. Those under eighteen years of age cannot work in some dangerous jobs. These include logging, mining, and work with dynamite or dangerous chemicals. However, the allowable age for working in some other jobs is lowered. These include delivering newspapers, babysitting, or working in the family business.

While each state determines its own labor laws, there are guidelines from the federal government. Students may not work

Federal and state rules restrict the type of work teens can do and the hours they can work. Certain dangerous jobs are off limits to minors entirely.

during school hours. In general, students may not work more than forty hours per week during the summer or more than eighteen hours per week during the school year. They cannot work more than three hours per day. Students may work between seven A.M. and seven P.M. during the school year. Minors may not work "graveyard" (overnight) shifts. Each state has its own rules about how late teenagers can work during the summer. Usually it is no later than nine P.M. Many minors work later than this, especially in restaurants and cashier positions. Some states also place limits on age for door-to-door sales. Some have rules about minors working in the entertainment business, for instance, as actors or models.

Teens also have duties in the workplace. All employees need to understand the job and what employers expect of them. Employees must follow safety and workplace rules. And just as teens do not want their rights violated at work, it is also important that a teen not violate the rights of other employees. Harassment in any form is against the law. Employers may fire employees for drinking or using drugs. Respecting other employees and their rights will help support a positive, safe working environment for everyone involved.

Teens may find some of the employment laws unfair. The laws are in place to protect minors from unsafe and abusive work environments. Not that long ago, children worked twelve to fifteen hour days with little or no break. In very poor families, students dropped out of school so they could work. In other parts of the world, children still work very long hours with very little pay and in unsafe environments.

Some people believe that not allowing minors to work puts unnecessary financial stress on some families. Around the world, many families could not survive if the children did not work. But children who work full time are not able to go to school. This means they will have little chance of getting better paying work later on in life. It is a tough cycle. Labor laws involving children

This photo of boys working on a Maine farm was taken in 1940.
In those days, school schedules were built around the harvest,
and children contributed to their families' livelihood.

in the United States began in the nineteenth century to help
prevent this cycle. In most states, children are required to attend
school up to at least eighth grade. This helps ensure that most
children receive a basic level of education. The limits on hours
worked during the school year are in place to support education.
They help make sure that minors are able to continue their
education and work at the same time.

Teens who have dropped out of school are an exception to
some labor laws. They may work full time. They also have the

benefits that come with working full time. But wages for a person who has not finished high school are much lower than those who at least have a high school diploma. Unemployment rates are also much higher for those who have dropped out of high school. A 1997 report showed that only 36.1 percent of white high school dropouts working full time earned a wage above the poverty line. Only 6.8 percent of black dropouts reached this wage level.[2] While dropping out of school in order to work may seem like a good idea, in the long run it can cause more problems.

What Can I Do If My Rights Are Being Violated?

Workplace abuses take many forms. Each situation needs to be reviewed on its own. Most workplaces have complaint procedures in place for employees to use if there is a problem. Some employers have better complaint policies than others. These procedures should be included in the employee handbook, if available. Sometimes workplaces are small and informal, with no official complaint policy. How to deal with an issue depends on the work environment. Ideally, the first place an employee will turn to report or discuss a problem is his or her supervisor.

Anyone who suspects that an employer is not following the law has the right to report that employer to the proper authorities. Report workplace safety issues to OSHA or to the state's workers' insurance plan. Employers are required to post information on state insurance coverage and how to contact the agency. Check the phone book or an online search. Use "workers' compensation" and the state name for information on each state's workers' compensation plan. An employee may feel that the work environment is unsafe and may cause immediate danger. He or she has the right to refuse to work until the employer corrects the problem.

According to a 1997 publication, every year about seventy teens die from work-related injuries, and another seventy thousand are seriously hurt.[3] Agriculture and working alone with cash are the two most dangerous jobs for teens.[4] Teens working agricultural jobs have died or been seriously hurt from the tools used. Sadly, teens have also died working alone late at night in jobs that require working with cash. These types of jobs include restaurant and cashier positions. In 2000, an older employee got a bogus call to make a pizza delivery. On returning, he found a sixteen-year-old coworker shot to death.[5]

Every year about seventy teens in the United States die from work-related injuries, and another seventy thousand are seriously hurt.

Employees also have the right to join or organize a union, though not all employers support unions. In addition, no one needs to put up with sexual or other harassment on the job.[6] Harassment is when one person troubles or annoys another over and over or makes constant attacks. Sexual harassment occurs when these activities include comments about sexual activity, obscene remarks, or inappropriate touching.

If a supervisor is harassing an employee, the employee will need to take other steps in reporting it. Sometimes there is only one boss. In this case an employee may need to report a complaint to someone outside of the business. Problems can be discussed with an attorney. Other organizations to contact include the local job service (a state-run agency that assists people in finding jobs and explaining local labor laws), or the Better Business Bureau. Public reference librarians can also help find a proper agency. There are a number of organizations to contact about workplace issues. Employees can report health and safety issues to OSHA and the state's workers' compensation offices.

4 Consumer Rights

Teens spend billions of dollars every year on clothing, entertainment, and many other products and services. As a result, many suppliers of these goods are competing to earn those dollars. Some advertising specifically targets teens. Companies and brands try to hook a person at a young age. They may have a buyer for life, or at least for many years.

Advertising seeks to influence certain groups of people. Look at the difference between ads run during Saturday morning cartoons and those shown during prime time in the evening. Ads run during the middle of the day target stay-at-home moms. Ads run during programs for teens also attempt to attract and hook the audience.

Advertisers also target young buyers in not so obvious ways. Product placement is a common method. It puts products in television shows, movies, or video games in such a way that it seems to be a part of the setting but, in fact, is a method of advertising. Teens may be very aware of product placement, particularly when seen all over a video game. Even with this awareness, however, some teens fall victim to the advertising anyway. About a skateboarding game, one teen said, "You see a board in the game that you like and you want the equipment . . ."[1]

What about product placement in schools? Some large companies, such as those that make soft drinks, will help support school programs. They give schools money in return for the school putting vending machines in the school. Other companies are not quite as subtle. Some school "educational" tools use or show a product name or picture as part of the learning material itself. Why would a school choose to use such educational material? Companies provide the material for free or very low cost. Many schools' budgets are very tight. All consumers, not just teens, need to be aware of the methods used by advertisers.

When teens do decide to shop, they may face problems that most adults would not face. For example, retail employees or security officers may be more likely to keep an eye on a teen shopper than they would an adult shopper. While teens spend a lot in retail, business owners also see them as "problem" shoppers. The Mall of America, for example, put a policy in place in 1996 that required adult supervision of teen shoppers. This meant shoppers sixteen years of age or younger after 6:00 P.M. on Fridays and Saturdays needed an adult supervisor. The mall had become a "hang out" place. The mall security workers said the groups of teens were causing problems. The mall also developed a youth advisory council. This council worked with the mall staff to help figure out solutions for the kids that hung out at the mall. The council broke up in 2000, but it helped bring a voice to teen shoppers.[2]

What Are My Rights?

Minors do not have some consumer rights. This includes the right to enter into certain types of contracts. However, everyone has the right to not be conned by companies. Some sellers use unethical or illegal means of getting someone to purchase a product or service. Those who use illegal methods sometimes do not even have a product or service to offer. How can teens protect themselves against such practices? By knowing their rights, being aware, and using a healthy amount of skepticism when it comes to advertised promises that seem too good to be true.

As consumers, teens have the right to protect themselves against scams. To avoid scams, there are some things that teens need to be aware of. One is modeling scams. Ads may promise huge salaries and no upfront costs. But the contract given to the potential model asks him or her to pay hundreds of dollars for photos. The agency claims they will use the photos to promote the model. Legitimate modeling agencies, however, usually collect fees by taking a percentage of the fees paid to the model. Payment is made only after the agency has found work for the model. Many agents work this way. A valid modeling agency may ask for the model to pay for printing costs for a picture in the agency's book. The costs for this type of promotional material are much smaller and only cover the model's part of the printing cost. Potential models also need to be wary of agencies that claim to represent "all types of people." These agencies lead some people to believe that they may have a career in modeling when this is, in fact, unrealistic.

Teens can protect themselves against consumer scams by knowing their rights, being aware, and using a healthy amount of skepticism.

Teens interested in attending college should be careful not to fall for fake scholarship scams. Most real scholarship programs have strict guidelines and do not require an application fee.

Valid modeling agencies do not work with all types of people. Scam artists do, and they charge all types of people as well.

Fake scholarships are another area students may fall prey to. Most legitimate scholarship programs do not require an application fee. Most also have strict guidelines. Those that do require a fee and have loose procedures and requirements may be scams. It is also wise to avoid paying for scholarship-searching services. They are unreliable. If a scholarship program looks doubtful, a high school guidance counselor can help figure out if it is legitimate. So also can the financial aid office of the college or university.

Health scams are another area teens should be aware of. Media images are everywhere. The culture in the United States (and elsewhere) is obsessed with being thin and muscular. Numerous diet programs, pills, powders, drinks, and exercise programs promise super-fast results from using their products. Often these products are highly priced. They also often require that the user continue using the product for a long time. This ensures long-term sales. Some diet or exercise programs require that participants sign up for a long period of time. They also add on "hidden" costs after the fact. This can include paying for food, supplements, or equipment. Many clubs and services have the clients sign contracts that "lock" the person into the agreement for a long time. This could be years. The bottom line is that safe, legal pills do not make people thin. Almost all of the advertising for these products include fine print. The fine print says diet and exercise are an essential part of any weight loss program. It is not possible to "spot reduce" (lose weight or fat from one specific area of the body) through exercise. If a promise or claim seems too good to be true, it probably is.

What Are the Current Laws?

The law does require certain things of both buyers and sellers. Consumers need to report problems within a realistic amount

Rating systems for movies, CDs, and video games are guides to parents trying to choose appropriate items for children of particular ages.

of time. They also need to keep accurate records to prove how much, when, and how they paid for something (cash, check, or credit card). If copies of contracts and selling agreements list rules that the seller agrees to, the consumer should keep all that information on file.

What products do teens have the right to buy? Under pressure from the public and possible legislative action, the entertainment industry has voluntarily used rating systems for such items as video games, CDs, and movies. Various states have passed laws about selling certain products to minors. Movies are rated G for general audiences; PG, meaning parental guidance is suggested; PG-13, meaning some material may not be suitable for persons under the age of thirteen; R for restricted, meaning that anyone under age seventeen must be accompanied by a parent or adult guardian; and NC-17, meaning no one under age seventeen is allowed. Other types of entertainment use different rating systems. The Entertainment Software Rating Board (ESRB) rating systems are the most common for video games. These rating categories include Early Childhood, Kids to Adults, Teens, Mature, and Adult Only. The Recording Industry Association of America (RIAA) developed a parental advisory label for music. Television uses a set of guidelines ranging from Y, which is suitable for all children, to MA, which is for mature audiences only.

The nation continues to introduce legislation about how companies market products to minors. Laws also affect how businesses display products and the outcomes of selling unsuitable material to minors.

How are labels viewed? Minors and parents will probably continue to disagree about certain labels. Parents and the entertainment industry will probably continue to disagree on some labels as well. But a recent study showed that parents and the industry are coming together in some areas. Parents wanted rating labels. The media voluntarily used ratings (although under threat of possible legislative action). The study states, "When an entertainment industry rates a product as inappropriate for children, parent raters agree that it is inappropriate for children."[3] In other words, the entertainment industry and parents agree on what is, or is not, appropriate for minors. The study also explained the need for both parents and the entertainment industry to take responsibility for exposure to minors. The study, "A Validity Test of Movie, Television, and Video-Game Ratings," recommended that a universal rating system be developed. This would eliminate different rating systems for different forms of entertainment.[4]

What about shady companies and scams? Rules exist for them too. Sweepstakes, for example, must follow certain rules to remain legal. They must provide the entrant a business name and contact information. They must also list the estimated odds of winning, the dollar amount or retail value of a prize, and payment schedules. It is illegal for sweepstakes to announce that a person has won when he or she has not. Nor can they imitate government seals, or require a purchase to win. Be careful of high shipping costs on "free" items. These should sound a warning bell for the consumer.

Who Is Challenging the Law?

Some consumer laws that deal with minors are being challenged by groups that support youth rights. These include the American Civil Liberties Union, kidSPEAK!, and the Youth Free Expression Network. These groups work not only to change the labeling laws as they relate to music, movies, and games, but to have most age-related laws done away with. These people believe that consumer rights should extend to all people, regardless of age. They feel that young people can and should make their own decisions on how they spend their money. Some groups want to see all information and entertainment that is available for adults made available for minors as well. Groups such as these also push for a lower voting age, no drinking age, and so on.

On the other hand, many people support the labeling of music and games, as well as the limitations on adult material, such as pornography. They argue that they are protecting young people. Some people argue that violent games promote violent behavior. They point to such cases as the Columbine High School incident. The boys involved in the school shootings were also fans of violent games. People who support music labeling believe that sexually explicit lyrics and those promoting violence are not suitable for minors.

Critics of labels argue that minors should be able to choose what they watch and listen to, just as adults do. How do the artists feel about labels? According to the Teen Consumer Scrapbook, some artists say they appreciate the labels. The labels help families and also help prevent censorship of the artist's work.[5]

Do the labels work? A 2004 report by the Federal Trade Commission (FTC) stated that most industries were obeying the labeling guidelines. However, the report also said that the music, movie, and video game industries were still advertising the mature-rated products in ways that reached a younger audience—such as ads in magazines and TV shows that kids are exposed to.[6] The FTC's concern is that the industry is specifically targeting children despite labeling on those products saying they are for older consumers only. The industries may be complying with the voluntary guidelines. But a more important issue is whether or not minors are still able to purchase the products. The report states, "despite the existence of restrictive policies among some retailers, the Commission continues to find that teens can purchase rated or labeled entertainment products at a significant number of stores and theaters."[7]

Most stores will exchange defective products, since satisfied customers tend to come back and may also recommend the store to their friends.

What Can I Do If My Rights Are Being Violated?

Sometimes a product is defective or a customer needs to return an item. Most retailers want to keep customers happy. They will work with those who have complaints or wish to exchange or return merchandise. As long as the customer's complaints are reasonable, many businesses will exchange defective products or issue a return. Some will take back merchandise with no questions asked. Some businesses sell services rather than products. Many of these will work to correct the problem rather than risk an unhappy client. Upset clients tell their friends about the poor service.

Unfortunately, not all businesses are so easy to work with. How does one go about complaining? Teen Consumer Scrapbook is an online site for teens created by teens. It shares knowledge on commercialism and provides tips for teens when it comes to dealing with difficult businesses. Some of their suggestions include:

- Complain as soon as possible and be very clear with the facts of the issue. When writing, calling, or complaining in person, it is important to have all the information on hand to answer questions and present a case. Information that may be required are the date of purchase, amount of purchase, a receipt of purchase, serial and model numbers, warranty information, and other related information.

- If the first attempt is unsuccessful, try using a different approach. If the first complaint was through a phone call, for example, complaining in person or by a letter may have better results. (It can also help to ask to speak with a supervisor.)

- Ask for a specific remedy and time frame, and use a firm voice and words.

- Follow up after the complaint. If no action is taken to resolve the problem, further action may be needed.[8]

If the complaint is with a very large company, or is the result of a suspected scam, it may be necessary to start at a higher level. The Better Business Bureau and the Federal Trade Commission are two agencies that deal with consumer issues. They also provide a wealth of information for consumers on their Web sites. Suspected scams and other consumer complaints can also be reported to the state auditor's office.

Health Care   5

Parents have a responsibility to take care of their children's health needs and provide the healthiest environment possible. Unfortunately, this is not always easy, due to the high costs of health care and insurance as well as food and shelter. Sometimes a parent's failure to provide health care and a healthy environment for their children crosses the legal line. This can even result in parents' losing their rights to have their children live with them.

Two areas that can result in adults losing their parental rights are abuse and neglect. Abuse can be emotional or physical. It is difficult to prove emotional abuse to the point where a parent would lose rights. Physical abuse as it relates to parent and child occurs when the parent physically harms the child. This can include hitting or shoving. Sexual abuse occurs when an adult engages in sexual behavior with a minor. Neglect occurs when parents or caregivers do not meet needs of their children. This is usually intentional. In some cases, a parent's mental illness will cause them to neglect a child. Either abuse or neglect can result in the loss of parental rights.

Parents are required to meet their children's physical needs. They must also provide health care as needed. But can a teen seek health care without a parent's consent? Sometimes.

All patients, including teens, deserve to be treated with respect. Patients also have the right to see their records and have any confusing information explained.

Typically, many doctors and health care providers will not treat a minor without the consent of a parent or guardian. However, most states allow teens to seek medical care for certain issues. These include drug and sexual health issues, outpatient mental health, pregnancy care, and in some cases, abortion. These are serious issues that require immediate assistance. As a result, doctors do not deny care on the basis of parental consent.

If a teen's health is in immediate danger, doctors will give care without consent. An example of this is a serious accident where the patient will die or suffer serious injury if immediate medical care is not given. But in other less obvious cases, a doctor can provide care without a parent's consent. If a teen has a drug problem and seeks treatment, the parents do not need to be informed. A teen can also seek information on reproductive health and sexually transmitted diseases (STDs). But the lines become blurry when teens seek treatment for STDs, pregnancy, and abortions. The laws differ from state to state on whether parents should be notified or required to provide consent.

What Are My Rights?

Teens have the right to seek health care and get accurate answers to their questions. Medical care is not limited because of a person's race, religion, age, or gender. Seeking medical help without a parent may seem a little frightening. Even if a parent is not present, the teen, as the patient, deserves treatment with dignity and respect. If this does not happen, the teen may need to find another health professional or organization. The patient also has the right to ask to see his or her records and have any confusing information explained.

Many aspects of health care can be overwhelming. Patients are required to fill out forms, often more than one. Many procedures and conditions have long, confusing names. Teens have a right to know what they are signing. They also have the right to understand what all procedures and tests are, and what their purpose is. If a health care worker is not explaining things well, it is okay to ask to have the information repeated in "common" language. Often medical language does not make much sense. Health care workers need to explain medical terms in "real" words. (This happens to both teen and adult patients.) Once the patient fully understands the information, he or she has the right to refuse any medical procedures. Following tests or procedures, the patient has the right to know the results. While seeking medical treatment can at times feel intimidating, it is important to speak out and ask questions.[1]

What Are the Current Laws?

If a teen's health is in serious danger, he or she may seek medical treatment without parental consent. Special options are available for those seeking treatment for alcohol or drug dependency. Options are also available for those seeking treatment from abuse. Teens needing help for sexually transmitted diseases may seek medical care without the consent of a parent.

States have differing laws on when parents need to be informed or provide consent on health care issues. Minors may buy over-the-counter contraceptives just like any other consumer. In some states, minors may also be able to obtain prescription birth control methods without a parent's knowledge.

Girls who are seeking an abortion have special rights. *Roe* v. *Wade*, a 1973 landmark Supreme Court case, ruled about a woman's right to an abortion. It said a woman could make up her own mind about whether or not to seek an abortion during the first trimester of the pregnancy. Under the ruling, states could pass laws regulating abortion during the second trimester. States could also pass laws protecting the fetus during the third trimester and only allow an abortion when the mother's health or life was in danger. The ruling was controversial and remains so today. Naturally, arguments for or against abortion for minors have continued, much the same as arguments about abortion in general.

What are the laws? Some states allow a minor to seek an abortion without informing her parents and without obtaining their consent. Others require that parents must be notified, but do not require consent. Still others require consent. Obviously, this by its very nature requires notification. Arguments for each option are varied. Some people fear that if a teen must notify her parents (or parent; some states require only one parent be notified) or get consent then she will seek other, unsafe methods for aborting the fetus. People who support notification and consent feel that a pregnant teen is unable to make the decision on her own. They believe that parental involvement is in her best interest.

The Alan Guttmacher Institute reports regularly on state laws about minors and STDs, pregnancy, and abortion. According to the institute, as of December 1, 2004:

- 32 states require some parental involvement in a minor's decision to have an abortion.

  - 18 states require parental consent; 2 require both parents to consent.

  - 14 states require parental notification; 2 require that both parents be notified.

- All of the 32 states, except Utah, that require parental involvement have an alternative process for minors seeking an abortion.

  - 31 states include a judicial bypass procedure, which allows a minor to obtain approval from a court.

  - 6 states also permit a minor to obtain an abortion if a grandparent or other adult relative is involved in the decision.

- Most states that require parental involvement make exceptions under certain circumstances.

  - 27 states permit a minor to obtain an abortion in a medical emergency.

  - 12 states permit a minor to obtain an abortion in cases of abuse, assault, incest, or neglect.[2]

Minors may seek treatment for drug and alcohol use. When seeking treatment, the minor's records are kept confidential. This means that a parent cannot see the minor's records unless the minor gives written consent. The laws generally provide confidentiality. This is so that those with drug or alcohol problems will not be scared off from seeking treatment. However, a doctor can share a minor's records with parents under certain circumstances. For instance, parents can be notified if a minor's condition poses a threat to his or her life, or that of someone else, and if the doctor believes that informing the parents will reduce the threat. Finally, notification may be necessary if the minor is unable to make a good decision based on extreme youth or other mental or physical conditions.[3]

Minors may also seek mental health care without parental consent. There are two types of mental health care. One is

In life-threatening emergencies, minors may receive medical treatment without their parents' consent.

inpatient care, where a hospital or care center admits the patient. The other is outpatient care, where the patient receives treatment by visiting caregivers (like regular visits to the doctor). In most cases, minors can get this type of treatment without parental notification or consent. The age at which a minor can obtain mental health care treatment without parental involvement varies from state to state.

Pros and Cons of the Law

The laws about emergency situations, drug- and sex-related issues, and mental health issues exist because the states realize that these situations require immediate help. While some people do not like the laws, they are in place to protect young people. A minor's health is more important than the parents' wishes in some cases. Along with these laws is the need for confidentiality of medical records. The laws recognize that adolescents, particularly older teens, are at a point in their lives when they are making more and more decisions for themselves. Having the right to control some issues of personal health is important to this process. The laws also recognize that teens may need someone to talk to. This person must be someone that they can trust and whom they know will keep the conversations confidential. If a parent is not able to perform this role, or if a teen does not trust a parent, a health care provider may be able to give the information and support that a teen needs.

Abortion, in particular, is an issue that provokes many emotions. People feel very strongly about the issue. Some feel so strongly, in fact, that they have died for their beliefs. People who reject abortion under any situation reject it for teens as well. Some groups will continue to push for laws outlawing abortion. These groups do not support abortion regardless of the age of the mother.

Other people who are usually opposed to abortion may not be opposed, or may be undecided, when it comes to teens. Some people may be uncomfortable with abortion generally, but will support it if the mother's health is in danger. Some people may also support it in cases in which the mother is still in school, is unmarried, or is unable to care for a baby—all of which are more likely among teenagers than among older women.

There are also supporters of abortion who will continue to fight for keeping the practice legal. Many supporters worry about the effects of illegal abortions. They feel that women, and especially young girls, will find other means of getting an abortion. These other methods are dangerous. Debates on the

Teenage girls look at the results of a home pregnancy test. Laws concerning prescription birth control and abortion differ from state to state.

topic will continue. The age of the mother will also continue to be a factor in the discussions.

What Can I Do If I Need Medical Care?

A teen in need of medical care may need it quickly. How does one go about finding such care?

Each state has its own laws about health care and teens. A good place to start asking questions is a family doctor. If a doctor is not available, the public health and human services department can provide information. (See the phone book for numbers.) Many communities have public health clinics that can help a teen find proper information. An emergency clinic may also have information. School counselors can provide local resources, as can reference librarians. If there is a local college or university, the on-campus clinic may also be able to provide information and services for attending students. Many college students are still minors. Many colleges have programs and information to help young people in need.

The yellow pages are another good resource for finding agencies. Look under general terms such as "alcohol" and "counseling" to find treatment agencies and counselors who focus on family and/or child issues. A phone call can lead to much-needed information. Help *is* out there, and it *can* be found.

6   Drug Testing and Searches

Drug testing is an issue discussed more and more over the past couple of decades. Discussions involve not only schools but the workplace as well. Can a school or employer conduct drug testing legally? Is mandatory (required) drug testing constitutional? Should it be limited only to those persons suspected of drug use? And even then, does it violate the person's rights?

Many schools and workplaces have put into place drug testing rules. In the workforce, drug testing is often required for jobs that are potentially dangerous. Examples are logging, or those in which an employee is responsible for the lives or well-being of others, such as a commercial airline pilot. Some other jobs that involve a high level of responsibility or deal with confidential information may also require drug testing.

Schools face different situations. Should drug testing be limited to students who participate in athletics? Student athletes are much more likely to be injured if they are using illegal drugs. But is it fair to single out those students, rather than testing the entire student body? In one well-known case that took place in Vernonia, Oregon, the school had a mandatory drug testing policy for student athletes. Jimmy Acton and his parents refused to sign the release allowing for the test. Jimmy argued that there was no reason to suspect he may be using drugs. Therefore, he did not think he should be tested. The school did not allow him to participate in the sports program.

Jimmy and his parents took the case to court. His case eventually ended up in the Supreme Court. Jimmy argued that he had protection under the Fourth Amendment. This amendment protects against unreasonable search and seizure. Jimmy argued that the policy invaded his privacy rights. The school district argued that drug use was prevalent in the school. They believed that the drug testing rules were legal and would help keep the student population under better control. Ultimately, the Supreme Court upheld the school policy. It said student athletes had fewer expectations of privacy. They change clothes and shower in the locker room, for example. The Court held that, because of the way the school gave the test, the collection of the urine sample was a limited invasion of privacy. Lowering drug use by athletes was more important than the athletes' individual privacy rights.

The Court's ruling was decided in a six-to-three vote. Justice Antonin Scalia wrote the Court's opinion, joined by Chief Justice William Rehnquist and Justices Anthony Kennedy, Clarence Thomas, Ruth Bader Ginsburg, and Stephen Breyer. The Court considered many factors in the case. It found that random drug testing of student athletes was not a violation of privacy. The justices said that participation in athletics was voluntary. The school was concerned about a drug problem among students. They said the testing was a reasonable search. The justices also said that students were required to submit to vaccinations. Athletes also had to submit to physicals before taking part in the athletic program. Students were also regularly subjected to other personal tests, such as those for hearing and scoliosis (a condition of the spine). The justices said that "students within the school environment have a lesser expectation of privacy than members of the population generally."[1] The justices also discussed the negative affects of drugs. They said that random testing was for the overall good of the student population.

The dissenting justices included Sandra Day O'Connor, John Paul Stevens, and David Souter. They said that if the goal of the program was to keep the general student body under more control, the limited testing of just the athletes did not make sense. They argued that testing suspected drug users makes more sense. It is more in line with the law than random testing of all students, including those who have shown no signs of drug use. In other words, they argued that random testing of the entire student body, or even random testing among a specific group (such as athletes), tests students who have not given the authorities any reason to suspect drug use. This practice is a violation of those students' rights.

The dissenting justices said that random testing violates the rights of many more students than only testing those suspected of the offense. The justices said that in all other areas of the law, people do not undergo searches unless there is a suspected reason. They referred to situations outside of the school situation. They argued that this should be the case in schools as well. (This case occurred before September 11, 2001; searches of the public have increased since those terrorist attacks.) This would also reduce the number of students exposed to privacy violations. The justices believed that a random or mandatory policy of testing the entire student body was not necessary. In fact, they felt that mandatory testing of all students would be a violation of their rights. Drug testing should be limited to only those suspected of use. The results should be limited to only those persons who needed to know, according to the dissenting opinion.

The dissenting justices said that drug testing was different from other procedures required by the school district, such as vaccinations. The justices said that the purpose of vaccinations is not to find something that may lay blame on the student. A student who receives a vaccination will not feel as if he or she is suspected of wrongdoing. However, that is the only response a student can have when asked to submit to a drug test, the dissenting judges argued.

What Are My Rights?

Arguments about the constitutionality of drug testing often mention the Fourth Amendment to the U.S. Constitution. This amendment protects a person against unreasonable search and seizure. However, some personal constitutional rights are waived in the school setting for the greater good of the entire student body. It is under this principle that many courts, including the Supreme Court, have upheld many drug testing cases in schools.

Amendment 4: Search and Arrest Warrants

The right of the people to be secure in their persons, houses, papers, and effects, against unreasonable searches and seizures, shall not be violated, and no warrants shall issue, but upon probable cause, supported by oath or affirmation, and particularly describing the place to be searched, and the persons or things to be seized.

Does a student have the right to refuse a drug test? In the case of student athletes, one may refuse to take the test. This may result in not being able to participate in the sport. Because school athletics are not required, the drug testing rule does not interfere with the student's education.

If a drug test is performed, students have the right to have the test given in a respectful manner. A school official will supervise the test, following certain guidelines. In the Vernonia school case, the person supervising the test needed to stand away from the urinal for boys. For girls, the person waited outside the stall. The sample was tested for temperature to make sure it was fresh. Only one person supervised the test, and the student's privacy was protected as best as possible. These were the standards already used in Vernonia, which the Supreme Court supported.

The courts also said that once test results are returned, the student has the right to know the results. Due to possible errors, students must be allowed to take a second test if the first one is positive for drug use. If the second test comes back negative, then the case is dropped with no further action taken against the student. If the student is suspended from school following a positive test, the school needs to inform the student of the reasons for suspension. Students also have the right to know that their sample will only be used to test for drugs that are specified before the test. The sample cannot be tested for medical conditions or pregnancy, for example. In 1975, the case of *Goss v. Lopez* determined that before a student is suspended, he or she must be made aware of the reasons for the suspension and given notice. "Due process" refers to the fairness in which laws are carried out. The Fourteenth Amendment to the Constitution protects due process. This amendment defines citizenship and guarantees equal protection under the law for all citizens.

In an effort to curb the problem of illegal drugs, many schools require all students who participate in athletic programs to participate in random drug testing. The Supreme Court has upheld this requirement.

What Are the Current Laws?

So far, random drug testing for athletes, as well as students involved in other optional activities, has been upheld in courts, because those activities are voluntary. In 2002, the Supreme Court gave schools more authority to randomly test for drugs among students who are involved in competitive or optional activities.[2] In early 2004, President Bush announced plans to increase funding by $25 million for schools to use for random drug testing.

Amendment 14: Civil Rights

Section 1. All persons born or naturalized in the United States, and subject to the jurisdiction thereof, are citizens of the United States and of the state wherein they reside. No state shall make or enforce any law which shall abridge the privileges or immunities of citizens of the United States; nor shall any state deprive any person of life, liberty, or property, without due process of law; nor deny to any person within its jurisdiction the equal protection of the laws.

Random drug testing of all students and mandatory drug testing of all students or students involved in specific activities are not yet legal. Some believe that the United States is headed in that direction. In early 2004, a well-publicized raid on a school brought national attention. The raid took place at Stratford High School in Goose Creek, South Carolina. Its purpose was to find drugs. Police with guns and dogs entered the school. They searched students' persons, property, and lockers. While the incident did not directly involve drug testing, it drew national attention as the "war" on drugs continued. The American Civil Liberties Union filed a suit against the school on behalf of twenty families. They felt this was a gross invasion of privacy. No warrants were issued or warnings given to the students. It was deemed "unreasonable" by the parents. (And no drugs were found.)

Can schools search a student's person or possessions without a good cause? In 1985, the Supreme Court ruled on a case involving a fourteen-year-old girl. The assistant principal caught her and a friend smoking cigarettes in the school bathroom. Terry (known by her initials, T.L.O., in court documents) denied that she had been smoking. The assistant principal asked to see her purse. While looking through the purse, he saw some rolling papers, which he knew were used for marijuana. Upon a further search of the purse, the assistant principal found marijuana.

He also found an index card that listed people who owed Terry money.

The principal called Terry's mother and the police. At the police station, Terry admitted to selling marijuana at school. She was then charged. In response, Terry argued that the search of her purse violated her Fourth Amendment rights against unreasonable search and seizure. A juvenile court heard the case. It upheld the assistant principal's actions. Terry then appealed her case through the court system. The Supreme Court eventually heard the case. The Supreme Court said the assistant principal had reason to suspect that Terry was violating school rules. She had been caught smoking, and therefore the search for cigarettes in her purse was not unconstitutional. The rolling papers led to a reasonable suspicion that there might be drugs as well. As a result of this case, school officials can search a students' person and property if they have a reasonable suspicion that a student is breaking or plans to break school rules. The decision must be based on a number of factors, including the student's age, history of behavior, and school records.

> **Random drug testing for extracurricular school activities has been upheld in courts, because those activities are voluntary.**

Zero Tolerance

Cases like Terry's, and more disturbing situations such as school shootings, have led schools to become more cautious about what students bring into schools. This has led to zero-tolerance policies. With these policies, schools do not allow any violations of the rules, no matter how innocent. The idea is to create an atmosphere where the school will not tolerate violations of the rules. This is to enforce safety, and also to ensure equal treatment among students in the process. Zero-tolerance rules address all kinds of issues facing children in school. This includes weapons, sexual harassment, and drugs, both legal and illegal.

Under zero-tolerance policies, students can be suspended or expelled if they break the rules. Mitch Muller's case at the opening of this book is one example. Mitch and his friends may not have realized that the laser pointer they were playing with could have been mistaken for a small gun. But school policy did not allow *any* toys that resembled firearms, so the school expelled Mitch. The policies punish both major violations, such as bringing a gun to school, and minor violations, such as having over-the-counter medications, in the same manner.

Another criticism facing zero tolerance is the method in which the policies are enforced. "Due process" refers to basic rights, including substantive and procedural. "Substantive" rights are those that allow the individual the power to possess or to do certain things, despite the government's desire otherwise. These are rights like freedom of speech and religion. "Procedural" rights are special rights that say *how* the government can lawfully take away a person's freedom or property or life. Due process rights carry over to the school setting as well. Many cases involving zero tolerance have to do with due process. In the T.L.O. case, for example, Terry argued that the assistant principal violated her constitutional rights when he searched her purse. She argued the search violated her due process rights (even though all the courts disagreed with her).

Zero-tolerance policies grew out of a need to provide safe school environments. As long as schools continue to look for ways to reach this end, controversy over the methods will continue.

Who Is Challenging the Law?

How far should school policies go? Many believe that plans for schoolwide drug testing go too far. Some people argue that many policies, particularly those of zero tolerance, cross the line and violate rights. Students have been suspended or expelled from school for using legal medications. These include

Some schools have searched students as well as their belongings and lockers for forbidden materials.

over-the-counter medications such as Tylenol as well as prescription medications such as asthma inhalers. States have been working on bills to allow children to carry their asthma medications in school. An Intermountain Heath Care newsletter in August 2004 mentioned a new bill in Utah:

> Prior to the bill being passed, policies in Utah varied from school district to school district. In some schools, a student could be suspended or expelled for possession on [sic] any type of drug,

including asthma inhalers and medications. If a student was having an asthma attack, they would have to go to the main office to obtain their inhaler. This delay could create panic for the student and make their asthma attack more severe.[3]

Most people do not question the drug problem in the United States. Nor do they question that youth are at a risk for drug abuse. What is questioned is how the country is going about dealing with the drug problem and what schools are doing about it. It is difficult to determine exactly which policies go too far and violate students' rights to privacy and rights against unreasonable search and seizure. Does drug testing work and address the real problem? Some people believe that drug testing does not address the real issue. Good education about the harmful effects of drugs would do more good than random drug testing, they say. They argue that finding drugs in a urine test after the fact is not as useful as preventing drug use in the first place.

Not everyone views zero tolerance and strict drug testing policies as a violation of freedom. Drug abuse is common, and it causes many problems, not only within the school setting but also in one's personal life. For the good of society, some people argue that drug testing is one way to help keep drugs out of the schools.

But should a person's right to privacy and rights against unreasonable search and seizure be ignored because he or she is a middle or high school student? Supporters of student rights argue that these policies go too far. They argue that there are better ways to deal with drug problems. They recommend better education about drugs and their use rather than simply telling kids to "just say no" or using scare tactics. Just as with sex education, they argue, when teens know the specific facts, they are better able to make informed, reasonable, and educated choices.

What Can I Do If My Rights Are Being Violated?

The courts have allowed schools more freedom when it comes to testing for drugs. But it is still up to the community and school to determine if there is a need for such testing. Whether or not a student's rights have been violated depends on each situation. Many issues are at stake. These include why the testing is done, how the testing is done, and what is done with the results. If taking a complaint about illegal drug testing to school officials or the school board is not effective or satisfactory, seeking outside legal help may be necessary.

7   Intellectual Freedom

According to the American Library Association (ALA):

> Intellectual freedom is the right of every individual to both seek
> and receive information from all points of view without restriction.
> It provides for free access to all expressions of ideas through which
> any and all sides of a question, cause or movement may be
> explored.[1]

Earlier in American history, slaves caught reading or
learning to read were often severely punished. Why? A slave
who could read had access to information. And information
leads to knowledge. And knowledge, it is said, is power. And
power can be a dangerous thing.

Do teens have the right to access any information they are looking for? With the widespread availability of the Internet, all kinds of information are available. Anyone can put a Web site on the Internet. They can put out information, regardless of qualifications or knowledge of a subject. Some of it is accurate. Some of it is not. Should teens be prevented from viewing certain Web sites?

The gathering and transferring of information can be a touchy subject. This is particularly true when it comes to the Internet. Some people want to require some Web sites be made illegal for minors to access. Some sites are already illegal for minors (such as pornography Web sites). Web sites containing information on how to build a bomb or that show graphic violence may fall into this category. Some Web sites already require that those who enter the site be eighteen years of age. But many Web sites do not require users to verify age. Some people want public institutions, such as libraries, to block certain Web sites that may be offensive to children or teens. Yet there are those who worry, especially with the passage of the USA PATRIOT Act (Uniting and Strengthening America by Providing Appropriate Tools Required to Intercept and Obstruct Terrorism Act) in 2001, that the government's ability to track what types of information people look at is a violation of privacy rights.

The American Library Association has historically protected the rights of individuals to access information confidentially. The association has many concerns about the PATRIOT Act. Public libraries do not give out an adult patron's checkout history. They will only do this if required to by law, such as a court subpoena for such records. If anyone, including government personnel, is allowed to review a patron's history, for example, it could have serious results. Libraries have different policies on allowing parents to access their children's checkout history. Some allow it up to a certain age. Some do not allow it at all.

What if an abused child was looking into resources that could help him or her escape the situation? If the abuse came from a parent, and the parent was allowed access to the child's records, it could have serious results for the child. Some states are looking into legislation that would make it legal for parents to access their children's records.

The ALA feels that what a person reads is his or her own business. Because of this belief, many libraries do not use Web site blockers (filters) on their computers. Filters may prevent patrons from accessing certain types of content, such as pornography. But the filters may block inoffensive or informational sites as well. Filters work by looking for certain words. Someone seeking information on breast cancer, for example, could be denied access because of the word "breast." Some libraries use blocking software only on computers located in children's sections. Others do not use blocking software at all. It is illegal for a patron to expose a minor to sexually explicit material. If a person is caught doing so, he or she can face criminal charges. Decisions on Web site blocking have created many arguments. The arguments are likely to continue.

As the Internet has gained in popularity and become more accessible, legislators have introduced numerous acts with the purpose of protecting minors from unsuitable content. The Communications Decency Act (CDA) was introduced in 1996 and struck down by the Supreme Court in 1997 as a violation of the First Amendment. The CDA attempted to ban obscene or indecent information on the Internet. In *Reno* v. *ACLU*, the Supreme Court found that free-speech principles applied to the Internet. The Child Online Protection Act (COPA) was passed in 1998. Its purpose is to prohibit businesses from distributing "harmful" material to minors (such as pornography). The Children's Online Privacy Protection Act (COPPA) went into action in 1998. It prohibits commercial Web sites from obtaining personal information from children under thirteen years of age. The Children's Internet Protection Act (CIPA) "requires libraries and schools to install filters on their Internet computers to retain federal funding and discounts for computers and computer access."[2] This legislation went into effect in 2000. While it is not required, some libraries feel they have no choice but to follow the rules in order to get the funding they need.

What Are My Rights?

The Constitution does not specifically list the right to privacy. It is implied in the Fourth Amendment and, more recently, the Ninth.

Amendment 9: Rights Retained by the People

The enumeration in the Constitution, of certain rights, shall not be construed to deny or disparage others retained by the people.

While the right to privacy is not specifically mentioned in the Ninth Amendment, the courts have argued that this right is implied. The Ninth Amendment was created as a broad amendment to cover "rights of the people," and the right to privacy falls under this category. The Supreme Court rarely mentioned the Ninth Amendment until the 1960s, when it was used in a case in 1965 involving privacy for married couples (*Griswold* v. *Connecticut*). Since that time, the Ninth Amendment has been used in other cases about the right to privacy as well.[3]

The Supreme Court has repeatedly made decisions that protect the privacy of individuals. But has it gone too far? Some people worry that the Court relies too much on the Ninth Amendment. They worry this allows the Court to invent rights and that it is gaining a power it was never meant to have. Traditionally, up until the mid-1960s, the courts used the Ninth Amendment only in conjunction with other amendments. This is because the wording of the Ninth is so vague. However,

Some libraries use blocking software on their computers to make sure children cannot access inappropriate sites. However, this practice can limit the rights of adults.

just because some issues have been argued and won using the Ninth Amendment does not mean that everyone agrees that they are rights.

Intellectual freedom issues fall under the First Amendment. Minors, like adults, have First Amendment rights. This includes the right to obtain information. Where information is obtained and how may vary from state to state and school to school. Minors have the right to look for information on a wide range of topics. Some people do not believe that minors should have access to all types of information, even if it is legal for them to do so. This includes information on sex, reproduction, and birth control. "Censorship" means keeping specific information from a person or group of people. Throughout history, information has been censored by many different people and institutions. Governments have censored information, as have other organizations and groups. Parents may censor information from their children, such as information on birth control. Our laws say they have the right to do so until the child reaches the legal age of eighteen. Parents may also require that their children be excused from reading certain material or be exposed to lessons in school that they find offensive. This includes sex education classes and books that have been banned by some groups.

As far as books and Internet censorship are concerned, school libraries are more likely to limit information than a public library. Schools may limit information that does not support the goal of education. This broad definition can lead to censorship of material considered inappropriate, as opposed to simply "educationally unsuitable." Schools may restrict some information if it is seen as "vulgar." Who decides what is "educationally unsuitable" or "vulgar"? That is up to school officials. Outside opinions from the community or parents may also influence a school's decisions.

In 1982, in the case of *Island Trees* v. *Pico*, the Island Trees Union Free School District (in New York) Board of Education acted to have some books banned from the school library. They considered the books to be "anti-American, anti-Christian, anti-Semitic, and just plain filthy."[4] Parents from the community disagreed with the decision, and the case eventually made it to the Supreme Court. The Supreme Court argued that "the Board could not restrict the availability of books in its libraries simply because its members disagreed with their idea content."[5] The Court found that the board's actions were in violation of students' First Amendment rights.

Some groups will continue to push to have books banned. A recent example is the Harry Potter series because of the wizardry and witchcraft in the books.

What Are the Current Laws?

Laws about access to information and a person's records vary from state to state. When needed, the Supreme Court has weighed in on a few issues.

Minors' rights to receive information have been limited in two ways. The Supreme Court has given public schools the right to decide whether to keep certain information in the school or school library. The school can decide if the information is "educationally unsuitable" or "pervasively vulgar." These are, of course, broad terms and are open to debate as to what they actually mean. The purpose of these terms is to leave the issue of information access up to the school officials. This is to prevent one person's opinion (such as a teacher's) from unfairly affecting the decision. On the other hand, this ruling gave schools a significant amount of control over the students' access to ideas and information.

The law says that parents may keep certain kinds of information from their children and may limit what they read.

Public libraries are not under the same restrictions as school libraries. Most public libraries aim to stock the shelves and provide patrons with information that is geared towards the library's patronage. This can vary from library to library. Sometimes a public library chooses not to have particular information. This is often not out of a desire to keep information from the public (censorship), but more likely to be a result of funds and space available for material. Whether or not there seems to be a community demand for such information also affects the decision.

The Supreme Court has restricted information to minors on information that states may determine is "obscene" for minors but not for adults. This includes stores selling obscene material to minors. It also includes any other way in which minors may obtain obscene material outside the home. Many states have adopted "harmful to minors" statutes that dictate the laws on information access. It may be fairly easy for a school not to purchase obscene books or magazines. Much of the controversy surrounding obscene material is the result of Internet access. The Internet can be a great learning tool, but it also has material that is not suitable for minors.

Many people support the idea of censorship in the form of filtering programs on computers. They believe that it is a necessary safety measure to protect minors. Some useful information may be blocked. The overall usefulness of the filters is worth the loss of some information, they say. They believe that filters do more good than harm.

Others argue that the filters block too much information, even for minors. They say it takes the idea of protection too far. Some words commonly blocked by filters include those that may help minors find important health information. This could include sexual health information or information on controversial topics such as homosexuality. Some teens may be in desperate need of help and have no other source of accurate information. Filters may prevent them from finding it.

Talk About It

In reference to the war on terrorism and the PATRIOT Act, Kari Lydersen writes, "The fear of government surveillance, including the provisions in the Patriot Act that allow internet monitoring and spying on what people obtain from libraries and bookstores can't help but have a stultifying effect on the free exchange of information."[6]

Those who support censorship tend to be concerned citizens who fear that some materials may harm children or teach them things that could be harmful. Censored material often involves

Some people believe teens should make their own decisions about what to read. Others think they should be protected from some types of material, and have campaigned to have books removed from school libraries.

sexually related content, offensive language, or potentially dangerous information, such as how to make bombs. Following the shootings at Columbine High School in Littleton, Colorado, in 1998, many people became more concerned about the information available to minors on the Internet. Columbine killers Eric Harris and Dylan Klebold found information on the Internet that they used to make pipe bombs.[7] Supporters of censorship argue that tragedies like this could be lessened if kids do not have access to this type of dangerous material.

Those who argue against censorship believe that people have the right to make their own choices about what they read and see.

They also argue that it is not up to the authority of certain people, groups, or the government to determine what should be taught in schools. Sex and drug education, for example, often fall into censorship issues. Those who oppose such education believe that it will only teach children how to use drugs or encourage them to have sex. These groups recommend "just say no" drug campaigns and "abstinence-only" sex education programs. Those who oppose such censorship argue that some minors will experiment—or at least seek information—no matter what. Having accurate information gives them the tools they need to make wise decisions rather than relying on friends or assumptions. They argue, for example, that abstinence programs provide inaccurate or limited information on pregnancy and sexually transmitted diseases and therefore leave teens at a disadvantage.

What Can I Do If My Rights Are Being Violated?

The American Library Association (ALA), in the article "What You Can Do to Oppose Censorship," lists a number of things people can do to fight censorship.[8] Another organization, kidSPEAK!, on their Web site page, "What Can I Do?" also lists ways in which minors can get involved to fight for intellectual freedom.[9] The following information is based on these lists.

For those who wish to oppose censorship (and not everyone does), a good place to start is the local library. Many libraries, including some school libraries, oppose censorship. Is it possible to fight censorship without breaking the law? Yes. Libraries do not support illegal activities. This includes exposing minors to inappropriate sexually explicit material. Nor do many libraries enforce the idea of censorship. Some help deal with the Internet issue by placing computers in the children's and young adult areas close to the librarians' desk. This discourages patrons from viewing

> For those who wish to oppose censorship (and not everyone does), a good place to start is the local library.

inappropriate material in the children's section of the library. Knowing the importance of intellectual freedom, and passing that knowledge on to others, is one way to support intellectual freedom at the library.

Even though minors may not vote, they do have the right and ability to contact people in decision-making jobs and government officials about issues that are important to young people. Contacting library and school boards, local media, and elected officials is one way to get an opinion out there and be heard. If a school is considering censoring certain information, students can ask to speak at one of the school board meetings to express opinions—either opposing or supporting the idea. Writing letters to the school and local papers may also be an option. A letter to the editor is an easy, brief way to get an opinion heard.

Keeping informed about issues related to intellectual freedom is also important. Following the news is a way to get information about what is going on at the local, state, and national levels.

Many people, including many minors, support censorship of some material. The First Amendment grants the right to personal opinions to all people. Teens can apply all the tools listed here to any issue regarding freedom of expression. Regardless of opinions, maintaining current information on the issues is important. It is difficult to take a stand without knowing all sides of an issue. Contacting government officials, writing letters, and developing campaigns to support a goal are all methods used to make a public statement.

Many groups are dedicated to preserving intellectual freedom rights, regardless of the positions. These groups feel that all opinions and voices can and should be heard. Joining such a group is a good way to get involved. Starting a group is another option. If a school is debating censorship issues, forming a student group to discuss issues and speak out is one way to take action.

Termination of Parental Rights and Emancipation

Every child has the right to live in a safe environment, free from abuse and neglect. Does this mean it always happens? No. Too many children grow up in unsafe homes. They suffer abuse, neglect, poverty, and a lot of other problems. Some of the larger issues related to parental rights have to do with abuse and neglect. These are serious issues, and a teen who finds himself or herself in a troublesome situation has the right to seek help. Finding that help may seem difficult or scary, but help is available. One way these problems are sometimes handled is through termination of parental rights (TPR), in which a court takes away the parents' rights to make decisions about a child. Some forms of abuse that may lead to termination of parental rights are outlined below.[1]

Physical abuse of children can range from spanking to beatings and more. Parents do this sometimes out of anger, sometimes to punish a child, and sometimes for no obvious reason. The law allows some forms of corporal (physical) punishment. Parents can take this too far and engage in abuse. Some cases of corporal punishment have gone to court. The rulings vary depending on each case. Some types of spanking, for example, are legal, and some are not.

According to a child advocacy organization, emotional abuse in the parent/child relationship occurs "when an adult continually hurts a child's feelings by calling names, using put downs, insults or humiliation."[2] Emotional abuse may not seem as serious as physical abuse. In reality, its effects can last a long time and be very damaging.

Sexual abuse in the parent/child relationship or an adult/child relationship occurs when the adult engages in sexual activity with the child. In these situations, the older person pushes inappropriate, unwanted, nonconsensual sexual behavior on the child. This unwanted behavior can include touching, kissing, fondling, nudity, and intercourse. There is a difference in the amount of power held by the people in the relationship, with the adult holding power over the child.

Statutory rape occurs when one person over a given age has sex with a person under the age of consent. (This is the age at which a person can legally consent to have sex, and it varies from state to state, with sixteen the most common.) Even if the younger person agrees to have sex, it is still a form of rape under the law, and the older person may face charges.

Neglect occurs when a caretaker deprives a child of basic needs. This can include physical, emotional, or educational needs. Physical needs include such things as food, water, clothing, and shelter. Emotional needs are love, attention, and protection. According to U.S. law, children also have a right to an education, which parents must meet.[3]

An abused person needs to find help immediately. Help may be in the form of assistance from a friend or a person in authority. Report any abuse to someone who can help. A school counselor can help direct a teen to the proper resources, as can a clergy member, or teacher. The state's department of public health and human services can provide help. The phone book may list a child abuse hotline.

Emotional abuse consisting of continual insults and humiliation can result in the termination of a parent's rights.

The Law

Parents who abuse or neglect their children can face criminal charges and be forced to give up their parental rights. Sometimes parents will give up the rights to their children voluntarily. If the charges are serious enough, the parent or parents may go to jail for their actions. When a parent loses parental rights, the children need a new home. Termination of parental rights is a legal procedure that makes adoption possible for the child or children without the consent of the birth parents. Before this occurs, children are sometimes put in foster care. This is when a family volunteers to care for the child until a permanent adoption can take place. Foster parents must go through a training program and be approved by the state. When children are in foster care, they remain in the foster care system until the state determines it is safe for them to return home. If it is not, the children will then be eligible for adoption. Sometimes foster parents adopt the children they have been caring for. Other relatives, such as grandparents or aunts and uncles, may take in the children, depending on the situation.

> When a minor is emancipated, it means that his or her parents are no longer responsible for providing food, shelter, health care, education, or any other basic needs. The law views the emancipated minor as an adult.

The laws on TPR vary greatly from state to state and the social welfare systems that each state has in place.

What Are My Rights?

If a teen is in trouble and needs to leave home, for a night or for an extended period of time, there may be more than one option, depending on the community. Youth shelters, if available, may allow a teen to stay overnight, but may require a parent's permission to do so. Children in serious trouble may be placed in temporary foster care until a long-term plan can be arranged if needed.

Speaking with a school counselor, trusted adult, or member of the clergy may help a teen determine possible solutions for seeking help. The yellow pages in the phone book may list local community groups that work with minors (see "adolescents" and related terms, or look under "counseling").

Emancipation

Most teens have probably thought about "divorcing" their parents at one time or another. While the idea may sound like a perfect solution, the reality is quite different. The term "emancipation" is often confused with the true meaning. It is not exactly like getting a divorce.

Under normal circumstances, parents are responsible for their child until he or she reaches the legal age. When a minor is emancipated, it means that his or her parents are no longer legally responsible for the minor. In other words, the parent is no longer responsible for providing food, shelter, health care, education, or any other basic needs. The parent has no legal or financial duties to an emancipated child. An emancipated teen is legally responsible for him- or herself. The law views the minor as an adult.

A judge will not grant emancipation just because a teen does not like the rules at home. The courts grant parents a lot of freedom when it comes to raising children. Unless a child is in danger, he or she is subject to the parents' rules until reaching legal age. Emancipation can occur a few different ways before a person reaches eighteen. A minor can marry (laws vary state by state in regards to age), join the military, or obtain a court order by proving that he or she is living on his or her own and is financially independent. The court will review all the information and make a decision.

Emancipation is a big decision. While it may be the right choice for some young people, emancipated teens are more likely than others to drop out of school and to become homeless.

Some states, such as California, offer simplified procedures for emancipation. These allow for parental consent and speed up the process. The minor must show that he or she is at least fourteen years of age, is financially independent, and is living apart from his or her parents. While this process is easier, an emancipated teen may be more likely to end up homeless or drop out of school. Emancipation is a decision that requires serious thought. It may be the right choice for some, but not all.

An emancipated teen faces schoolwork, employment, rent, medical expenses (which are particularly high, especially if no insurance is available), utilities . . . the list goes on. Even some people over the age of eighteen do not face all of these issues immediately after reaching the legal age. Many parents support their children into their twenties and sometimes afterward.

What Does It Mean?

What exactly does emancipation mean? It means that a minor is an adult according to the law. Does the minor have all the same rights as an adult? Not quite. Minors must still follow the law. A teen may not purchase tobacco products or drink until reaching the legal age. An emancipated minor cannot vote. Emancipated teens must also follow child labor laws.

How does one start the emancipation process? The child files an emancipation petition or has a lawyer file the petition. A judge reviews the case and makes a final decision. Emancipation usually cannot be undone, so careful consideration is required. Talking with a counselor and/or a lawyer may help a teen make a sound decision.

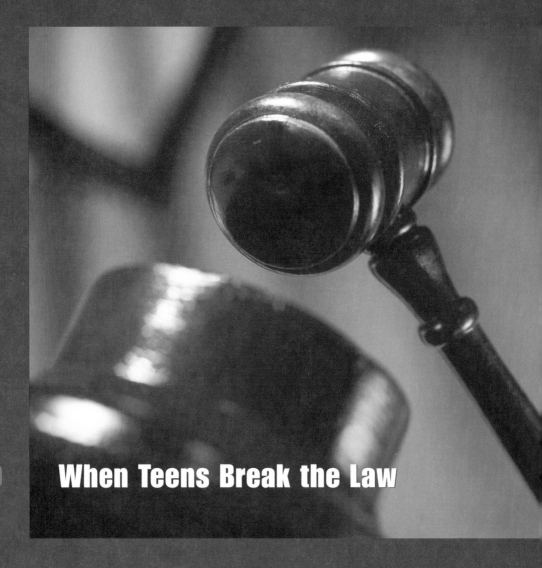

9

When Teens Break the Law

Some of the issues discussed already show what can happen if a teen breaks the rules at school. But what can happen when teens break the law? As with all other issues mentioned here, the laws vary from state to state. This is an overview of some general legal information that affects teens.

The United States Constitution allows each state to determine its own laws. The only rule is that the laws must be in compliance with the Constitution. As a result, punishment for the same crime can differ from state to state. The age at which a minor may be tried as an adult for a crime may also vary. One state may charge the offender as a juvenile while another state may charge the offender as an adult for the same crime.

Minors do have rights under the United States Constitution. However, their rights are more restricted than those of adults. For example, minors cannot vote or sign contracts. And while the Bill of Rights guarantees the freedom of speech, minors do not always have this right—for instance, when they are in school.

Until very recently, minors who were charged with breaking the law had very few of the due process protections given to adults. For instance, they did not have the right to have an attorney, to confront their accusers in court, to have a jury trial, to refuse to testify in their trial, or to appeal a verdict. This was because the purpose of the youth court system was to rehabilitate and teach young people rather than punish them. Experts believed that this would be more likely in an informal system in which judges had a great deal of discretion to decide cases and sentences.

> Until very recently, minors who were charged with breaking the law had very few of the due process protections given to adults, such as the right to an attorney or a jury trial.

In 1964, a fifteen-year-old boy in Arizona named Gerald Gault was arrested for making a prank phone call (including indecent remarks) to a neighbor. Gault was never read his rights, was never formally charged, did not have an attorney at his hearing, and was not allowed to confront his accuser in court. Despite all this, Gault was tried and sentenced to six years in a state juvenile detention facility. The case was eventually appealed to the Supreme Court, which in 1967 ruled for Gault. The Court said that because children who are charged with crimes faced many of the same consequences as adults, they should have the same right to due process.

Juvenile Court

Currently, a teen has the same legal rights as an adult during the arrest process. The Miranda warning is read by the police to suspects during an arrest. This is the list of rights heard in television shows and movies that begins, "You have the right to remain silent." If police do not read a suspect these rights, a judge may dismiss a case.

Juvenile court is a separate legal system that deals with legal issues affecting minors. In most states, the juvenile court system deals with those up to the age of eighteen. The juvenile court handles many issues. These include adoption, parental abuse and neglect, mental and physical health issues (such as abortion), and delinquency (misbehavior). When the juvenile court hears delinquency cases where a minor is charged with breaking the law, in most cases the court will attempt to address the problem. "Rehabilitation" in the court system refers to processes that help people charged with a crime change their ways and become productive members of society.

Even in the most serious of cases, such as a murder trial, a juvenile court will likely determine if rehabilitation is a possibility. This takes place before trying the juvenile or determining if the minor will be tried in juvenile or adult court. Some states, however, have a system in place that automatically places a case in the adult court. This means that some states will try a juvenile in an adult court for murder or other serious crimes without considering other factors. In Wisconsin, for example, a law requires that children aged ten to sixteen who are charged with certain types of homicide are automatically sent to adult court.[1]

Being tried in juvenile court, however, does not mean that a minor will automatically get off easy for committing a crime. Sentences in a juvenile court range from jail time to probation. (Probation is a system that allows a guilty person to stay out of

A trial in juvenile court does not mean a young offender will get off easy. Some people are sentenced to probation, while others serve time in jail.

jail and report to a probation officer instead. Breaking the rules of probation can lead to imprisonment.)[2]

Serving Time

When teens are required to serve jail time, they usually go to a juvenile ward. Time in a juvenile ward differs from time in a regular jail. Time is devoted to the rehabilitative process.[3] Serving time in one of these places is not easy. It just means that the focus is different. It also keeps minors away from adult offenders who are serving time.

Juveniles can serve time in adult prisons if found guilty of serious crimes. A 2000 report published by the U.S. Department of Justice states:

> Concerned that the juvenile justice system may be ill equipped to handle youth charged with serious crimes and that the juvenile court may be too lenient in its punishment and control of such youth, many states have begun amending their criminal codes so that youth charged with certain crimes can be tried in adult courts and sentenced as adults.[4]

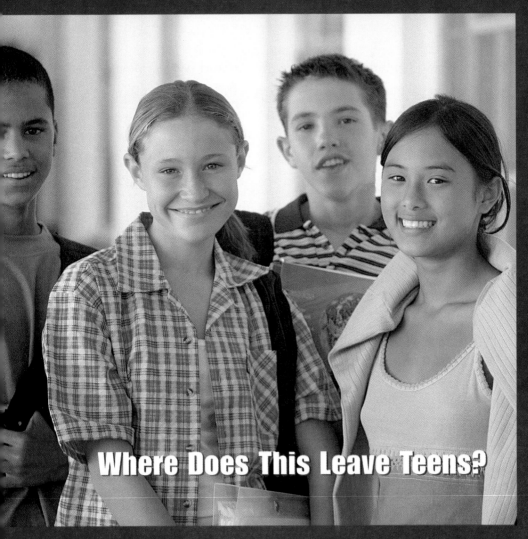

Where Does This Leave Teens?

10

The topics mentioned in this book are only a few areas about the rights of minors in the United States. Important issues affecting minors' rights cover a broad range of topics. Young people are concerned about and taking action for many other issues. Teens are speaking out on many topics. These include age requirements for voting and drinking, curfews, and more involved topics such as abuse and minors' rights around the world.

Having rights carries with it some responsibilities as well. It is a citizen's responsibility to know what his or her rights are.

Without this knowledge, a person will not know if they are being violated. He or she may also violate the rights of another. Having rights includes respecting the rights of others.

No one can know all of the laws inside and out (even attorneys have to do legal research). But having a basic understanding of the Constitution and the Bill of Rights helps ensure respect of all citizens' rights. The right to speak out is most effective when it is used intelligently. Having knowledge of basic human rights can help a person spot a violation of another's rights. It could even save someone else's life. Children's rights supporters feel very strongly about their role in helping speak for those who cannot. The same idea applies to everyday citizens. Knowledge is power. Being aware of various methods that some people use to exploit others can go a long way toward stopping abuses. For instance, knowing the signs of child abuse can lead towards getting a child proper help. Not allowing another person or company to take advantage of minors can lead to better human rights practices all around.

As with anything, keeping informed and taking action are ways to help ensure that rights remain constitutionally protected and enforced. For those who wish to seek change, taking action is the best way to deal with issues. Even for those who do not wish to take up a cause, knowing one's rights and keeping informed is necessary to fully function in school and in society.

Children in the United States have many rights that other children around the world do not. Around the globe, many crimes are committed against children. Even so, children's rights are still sometimes abused in the United States. Knowing about rights abuses is one thing. Doing something about it is another.

Young people do have options when it comes to taking action. Starting a rights group at school is one possibility. Getting involved in a local or national human rights group is another. Many organizations have information on the Internet about joining their organization as well as tips on starting a local group.

Writing articles and opinion pieces for both school and local papers is one way to discuss issues and draw attention to a problem. Writing local, state, and national decision makers is another way people get their voices heard. Even though minors cannot vote, they still have voices and can use them. Politicians are supposed to represent the people at large, not one particular group over another. Minors are important members of society.

Children in the United States have many rights that other children around the world do not. Around the globe, many crimes are committed against children.

Volunteering is another way to help support human rights activities. Check into local nonprofit groups for those who work for similar beliefs. Help others or work for a cause by volunteering.

While many people are working to speak for those who cannot speak for themselves, oftentimes, youth rights begin with youths. If a young person had not bothered to challenge the law, many youth rights would not be in place today. At times it may seem that minors do not have many rights. Some areas of the law will not change. But there is always room for some change, and there is only one way to go make change happen—by doing something about it.

Chapter Notes

Chapter 1   Do Teens Have Rights?

1. "State Court Agrees With Rutherford Institute, Reprimands School Officials for Expelling Student Over Toy Laser Pointer," *The Rutherford Institute,* June 7, 2000, <http://www.rutherford. org/about/recent_victories.asp> (December 17, 2004).

2. John Shattuck, "Civil and Political Rights in the United States," *U.S. Department of State Dispatch,* September 19, 1994, <http:// www.findarticles.com/p/articles/mi_m1584/is_n38_v5/ai_159302 15> (February 20, 2005).

3. Free The Children, "Children's Rights, Who Has Ratified?" 2003, <http://www.freethechildren.org/youthinaction/children's_rights_ who_has_ratified.htm> (February 28, 2004).

Chapter 2   Freedom of Expression

1. *Tinker* v. *Des Moines School Dist.,* 393 U.S. 503 (1969) 393 U.S. 503 *Tinker et al.* v. *Des Moines Independent Community School District et al., Certiorari* to the United States Court of Appeals for the Eighth Circuit, No. 21. Argued November 12, 1968, <http:// caselaw.lp.findlaw.com/scripts/getcase.pl?navby=case&court=US& vol=393&page=503> (February 29, 2004).

2. Associated Press, "Anti-Bush T-shirt banned at Michigan school," February 18, 2003, <http://www.cnn.com/2003/US/Midwest/02/ 19/antibush.tshirt.ap> (February 22, 2004).

3. "Student T-Shirts Censored in Time of War," *WireTap Magazine,* March 20, 2003, <http://www.alternet.org/wiretap15436> (December 11, 2004).

4. *Hazelwood School District* v. *Kuhlmeier,* 484 US 260 (1988), <http://www.wku.edu/Government/vhazel.htm> (February 23, 2004).

5. Oyez, U. S. Supreme Court Multimedia, "*Engel* v. *Vitale,*" n.d., <www.oyez.org/oyez/resource/case/111/abstract> (February 19, 2005).

6. FindLaw, "*Engel* v. *Vitale*," n.d., <http://caselaw.lp.findlaw.com/scripts/getcase.pl?court=US&vol=370&invol=421> (February 20, 2005).

7. *Engel* v. *Vitale*, 370 U.S. 421 (1962), <http://www.civnet.org/resources/teach/basic/part7/47.htm> (February 23, 2004).

8. *Lee* v. *Weisman*, 505 U.S. 577 (1992), Section (a), <http://tourolaw.edu/patch/Lee>.

9. Ibid., Section (b).

Chapter 3   On the Job

1. Steven Mitchell Sack, *The Employee Rights Handbook* (Warner Books: New York, 2000), pp. 9–14.

2. American Youth Policy Forum, "What's Really Happening with America's Out-of-School Youth?" April 18, 1997, <http://www.aypf.org/forumbriefs/1997/fb041897.htm> (February 22, 2005).

3. DHHS (NIOSH) Publication No. 97-132, June 1997, <http://www.cdc.gov/niosh/adoldoc.html> (February 23, 2004).

4. National Consumers League, "Clocking in for Trouble: Teens and Unsafe Work," n.d., <http://www.natlconsumersleague.org/childlabor/jobreport.htm> (December 8, 2004).

5. Ibid.

6. DHHS (NIOSH) Publication No. 97-132.

Chapter 4   Consumer Rights

1. Alissa Quart, *Branded: The Buying and Selling of Teenagers* (Cambridge, Mass.: Perseus Publishing, 2003), p. 98.

2. Rosalind Bentley and Terry Collins, "Teens: the lifeblood and headache of the mall," *Startribune.com*, n.d., <http://www.startribune.com/stories/1731/3137749-2.html> (December 8, 2004).

3. David A. Walsh and Douglas A. Gentile, "A Validity Test of Movie, Television, and Video-Game Ratings," *Pediatrics*, vol. 107, no. 6, June 2001, p. 1302.

4. Ibid.

5. Teen Consumer Scrapbook, "CD Parent Advisory Labels," n.d., <http://www.atg.wa.gov/teenconsumer/buyingG&S/cdlabels.htm> (February 23, 2004).

6. Federal Trade Commission, "Marketing Violent Entertainment to Children," July 12, 2004, <http://www.ftc.gov/os/2004/07/040708kidsviolencerpt.pdf> (December 10, 2004).

7. Ibid., p. 28.

8. Teen Consumer Scrapbook, "Consumer Complaints," n.d., <www.atg.wa.gov/teenconsumer/pages/buyingG&S/consumer comp.htm> (February 20, 2005).

Chapter 5 Health Care

1. Jefferson County Department of Health, Birmingham, Alabama, "Teens' Consumer Health Rights," n.d., <http://www.jcdh.org/default.asp?ID=128> (February 28, 2004).

2. The Alan Guttmacher Institute, "Parental Involvement in Minors' Abortion," *State Policies in Brief, as of December 1, 2004,* <http://www.guttmacher.org/statecenter/spibs/spib_PIMA.pdf> (December 11, 2004).

3. Rebecca Gudeman, "Federal Privacy Protection for Substance Abuse Treatment Records: Protecting Adolescents," July–September 2003, <http://www.youthlaw.org/downloads/substance_abuse_records.pdf> (December 11, 2004).

Chapter 6 Drug Testing and Searches

1. *Vernonia School District* v. *Acton,* 515 U.S. 646 (1995), <http://www.oyez.org/oyez/resource/case/626/> (January 11, 2005).

2. Office of National Drug Control Policy, "What You Need to Know About Drug Testing in Schools," n.d., <http://www.whitehousedrugpolicy.gov/pdf/drug_testing.pdf> (February 23, 2004).

3. Intermountain Health Care, "Managing Asthma," vol. 3, issue no. 3, August 2004, <http://www.ihc.com/xp/ihc/documents/hp/asthmanewsaug04.pdf> (December 11, 2004).

Chapter 7 Intellectual Freedom

1. American Library Association, "Intellectual Freedom and Censorship Q&A," n.d., <http://www.ala.org/ala/oif/basics/intellectual.htm#ifpoint1> (January 11, 2005).

2. American Library Association, "CPPA, COPA, CIPA: Which Is Which?" 2004, <http://www.ala.org/ala/oif/ifissues/issuesrelatedlinks/cppacopacipa.htm> (December 13, 2004).

3. FindLaw, "U. S. Constitution: Ninth Amendment," n.d., <http://caselaw.lp.findlaw.com/data/constitution/amendment09/#f5> (February 20, 2005).

4. *Board Of Education* v. *Pico,* 457 U.S. 853 (1982), abstract, n.d., <http://www.oyez.org/oyez/resource/case/1060/> (December 13, 2004).

5. Ibid.

6. Kari Lydersen, "Censorship Reaches Ridiculous Extremes," *AlterNet.org,* March 13, 2003, <http://www.alternet.org/story.html?StoryID=15368> (February 28, 2004).

7. "Did Cops Miss Columbine Tip?" *CBSNews.com,* October 30, 2003, <http://www.cbsnews.com/stories/2004/02/26/national/main602339.shtml> (December 13, 2004).

8. American Library Association, "What You Can Do to Oppose Censorship," n.d., <http://www.ala.org/Template.cfm?Section=basics&Template=/ContentManagement/ContentDisplay.cfm&ContentID=24792> (February 28, 2004).

9. kidSPEAK!, "What Can I Do?" <http://www.kidspeakonline.org/whatcanido.html> (February 29, 2004).

Chapter 8 Termination of Parental Rights and Emancipation

1. Laurie A. Couture, "General Information on Child Abuse and Neglect: Types of Abuse and Neglect," *ChildAdvocate.org,* 2003, <http://www.childadvocate.org/1d_types.htm> (February 29, 2004).

2. Ibid., <http://www.childadvocate.org/4c.htm> (February 29, 2004).

3. Ibid.

Chapter 9   When Teens Break the Law

1. Milwaukee Journal Sentinel, "Suspect, 10, May Become the
   Youngest Ever Charged," October 3, 2002,
   <http://www.cjcj.org/press/suspect.html> (December 13, 2004).
2. Legal Dictionary online, "probation," 2003–2004, <http://www.
   thelegaldictionary.com/legal-term-details/Probation> (December
   13, 2004).
3. Center on Juvenile and Criminal Justice, "Intro to California's
   Juvenile Justice System; Life as a Juvenile Ward," n.d., <http://
   www.cjcj.org/jjic/intro.php#ljw> (December 13, 2004).
4. U.S. Department of Justice, Office of Justice Programs, Bureau
   of Justice Assistance, James Austin, Kelly Dedel Johnson, Maria
   Gregoriou, Institute on Crime, Justice and Corrections at
   The George Washington University and National Council on
   Crime and Delinquency, "Juveniles in Adult Prisons and Jails,
   A National Assessment," October 2000, <http://www.ncjrs.org/
   pdffiles1/bja/182503.pdf> (December 13, 2004).

Glossary

amendment—Article added to the U.S. Constitution.

article—Separate clause or portion of a document.

Better Business Bureau—Agency that reports wrongful business practices.

Bill of Rights—The first ten amendments to the Constitution.

censor—A person who examines printed matter, movies, news, etc. to suppress parts on the grounds of obscenity, security, etc.

contraceptives—Means and methods to prevent pregnancy.

Convention on the Rights of the Child (CRC)—A list of articles developed by the United Nations in 1989 outlining rights specific to children.

defamation of character—A false statement that is intended to damage another person's character or otherwise cause harm.

due process—The principle that the state must use fair procedures when it acts to limit a person's life, liberty, or property.

emancipation—Becoming legal in the eyes of the law before reaching legal age (eighteen).

ERSB—Rating standard-setting body for video games.

Fair Labor Standards Act—The 1938 legislation that dictated areas of labor law, including child labor.

Federal Trade Commission—U.S. government agency dealing with consumer issues.

harass—To trouble and annoy continually.

hate speech—Hateful or derogatory speech aimed at another person or group of people; it is directed at people because of membership in a minority group, sexual orientation, etc.

Internet filters—Programs designed to block users from viewing Web sites containing certain words.

minor—Anyone under the state-defined legal age.

Occupational Safety and Health Administration (OSHA)—A U.S. government agency that regulates workplace safety.

ratify—To confirm or accept by formal consent, signature, etc.

Recording Industry Association of America (RIAA)—The organization that developed the Parental Advisory Label for explicit lyrics in music.

sexual harassment—Harassment involving sexual language, touching, or other inappropriate sexually related behavior.

slander—A false and hurtful statement about another.

Supreme Court—Highest court in the United States; deals with constitutional issues.

Universal Declaration of Human Rights (UDHR)—Declaration of the United Nations put into effect in 1948 that lists basic human rights.

For More Information

Free Expression and Censorship

The American Library Association
1301 Pennsylvania Avenue NW
Suite 403
Washington, DC 20004-1701
(800) 941-8478
(202) 628-8410

American Civil Liberties Union
25 Broad Street, 18th Floor
New York, NY 10004

National Coalition Against
  Censorship
275 Seventh Avenue
New York, NY 10001
Tel: (212) 807-6222
Fax: (212) 807-6245

Health

Center for Disease Control
Centers for Disease Control
  and Prevention
Public Inquiries/MASO
Mailstop F07
1600 Clifton Road
Atlanta, GA 30333
(800) 311-3435
(404) 639-3534

Job Safety and Rules

Occupational Safety &
  Health Administration
200 Constitution Avenue NW
Washington, DC 20210
(800) 321-OSHA

Youth Rights

Amnesty International USA
5 Penn Plaza, 14th Floor
New York, NY 10001
Tel: (212) 807-8400
Fax: (212) 627-1451

National Youth Rights Association
PO Box 5882 NW
Washington, DC 20016
Tel: (301) 738-6769
Fax: (202) 318-8966

Juvenile Law

American Bar Association
740 15th Street NW
Washington, DC 20005-1019
(202) 662-1000

Center on Juvenile and
  Criminal Justice
1234 Massachusetts Avenue NW
Suite C1009
Washington, DC 20005
Tel: (202) 737-7270
Fax: (202) 737-7271

Further Reading

Hibbert, Adam. *Children's Rights.* North Mankato, Minn.: Sea-to-Sea Publications, 2005.

Jacobs, Thomas A. *What Are My Rights? 95 Questions and Answers About Teens and the Law.* Minneapolis, Minn.: Free Spirit Publishing, 1997.

Jacobs, Thomas A. *Teens on Trial: Young People Who Challenged the Law—and Changed Your Life.* Minneapolis, Minn.: Free Spirit Publishing, 2000.

Kowalski, Kathiann M. *Teen Rights: At Home, At School, Online.* Berkeley Heights, N.J.: Enslow Publishers, Inc., 2000.

Krull, Kathleen. *A Kid's Guide to America's Bill of Rights: Curfews, Censorship, and the 100-Pound Giant.* New York: Avon Books, 1999.

McGowan, Keith. *Human Rights.* San Diego, Calif.: Lucent Books, 2003.

Springer, Jane. *Listen to Us: The World's Working Children.* Toronto: Douglas & McIntyre, 1997.

Internet Addresses

American Civil Liberties Union
  <http://www.aclu.org>

Center on Juvenile and Criminal Justice
  <http://www.cjcj.org>

National Youth Rights Association
  <http://www.youthrights.org>

Index